# Revolution of AI and Machine Learning for Design and Automation

# Revolution of AI and Machine Learning for Design and Automation

*Edited by*
**R. Rekha**
**M. V. Suganyadevi**

*CWP*

This edition has been published by Central West Publishing PTY LTD, (ABN 13 683 898 722) Australia
© 2026 Central West Publishing PTY LTD

For more information about the books published by Central West Publishing PTY LTD, please visit https://centralwestpublishing.com

**Disclaimer**
Every effort has been made by the publisher, editors and authors while preparing this book, however, no warranties are made regarding the accuracy and completeness of the content. The publisher, editors and authors disclaim without any limitation all warranties as well as any implied warranties about sales, along with fitness of the content for a particular purpose. Citation of any website and other information sources does not mean any endorsement from the publisher, editors and authors. For ascertaining the suitability of the contents contained herein for a particular lab or commercial use, consultation with the subject expert is needed. In addition, while using the information and methods contained herein, the practitioners and researchers need to be mindful for their own safety, along with the safety of others, including the professional parties and premises for whom they have professional responsibility. To the fullest extent of law, the publisher, editors and authors are not liable in all circumstances (special, incidental, and consequential) for any injury and/or damage to persons and property, along with any potential loss of profit and other commercial damages due to the use of any methods, products, guidelines, procedures contained in the material herein.

NATIONAL LIBRARY OF AUSTRALIA

A catalogue record for this book is available from the National Library of Australia

ISBN (print): 978-1-922617-66-8

# Preface

This book provides a comprehensive exploration of recent trends in engineering, with a focus on the groundbreaking advancements shaping the future of technology. It is structured to develop knowledge and understanding of key research areas that are transforming industries and academia alike.

The chapters delve into emerging technologies such as Artificial Intelligence (AI), Machine Learning (ML), Big Data Analytics, and the Internet of Things (IoT). Each of these topics is presented by eminent researchers who are at the forefront of innovation in their respective fields. AI and ML, for instance, are revolutionizing problem-solving and decision-making processes across various sectors, from healthcare to manufacturing. Big Data Analytics is providing unprecedented insights by processing vast amounts of information, driving more informed and efficient decision-making. Similarly, IoT is creating interconnected systems, enhancing automation, and enabling smarter environments.

This book serves as a crucial resource for students, researchers, and faculty members who wish to explore the latest developments in these rapidly evolving fields. It provides both theoretical foundations and practical insights, making it an essential guide for those involved in cutting-edge research or seeking to apply these technologies in real-world engineering solutions. Whether used as a textbook or a reference guide, this book offers valuable knowledge to support innovation in Engineering Automation and related disciplines.

By addressing these critical topics, the book not only highlights the importance of these technologies but also encourages readers to engage with the current research trends and contribute to the future advancements in engineering.

# Table of Contents

# Chapter 1

## Harnessing Machine Learning for Advanced Engineering Solutions

**J. Eindhumathy[1] and C. Vennila[2]**
[1]Saranathan College of Engineering, India
[2]VSB Engineering College, India

## Abstract

Machine learning (ML) offers transformative physical modeling and simulation capabilities in the rapidly evolving engineering field. This chapter delves into various ML techniques that are revolutionizing engineering applications. We explore supervised, unsupervised, and reinforcement learning methods, highlighting their unique strengths and use cases in engineering. Through detailed examples, we demonstrate how these techniques enhance predictive accuracy, optimize system performance, and facilitate the design of complex engineering systems. This chapter aims to equip engineers with the knowledge to effectively integrate ML into their workflows, ultimately driving innovation and efficiency.

**Keywords**: Machine Learning, Engineering Applications, Supervised Learning, Unsupervised Learning, Reinforcement Learning, Predictive Modeling, System Optimization

## 1.1 Introduction

Integrating machine learning into engineering practice represents a major paradigm shift, enabling the development of more accurate, efficient, and adaptive systems. Traditional engineering models, while robust, often suffer from complex, nonlinear problems and huge data sets. Machine learning techniques, with their ability to learn from data and improve over time, provide a powerful tool to address these challenges. In this chapter, we introduce the fundamental concepts of machine learning and their concrete applications in various engineering disciplines. We aim to demonstrate the potential of these technologies to revolutionize the field by bridging the gap between theoretical ML concepts and real engineering problems [1].

Machine learning (ML) is a subfield of artificial intelligence (AI) that focuses on developing algorithms and statistical models that allow computers to perform tasks without explicit instructions. Instead, these systems learn patterns and make decisions based on data. The main goal of ML is to enable computers to learn from experience and improve their performance over time.

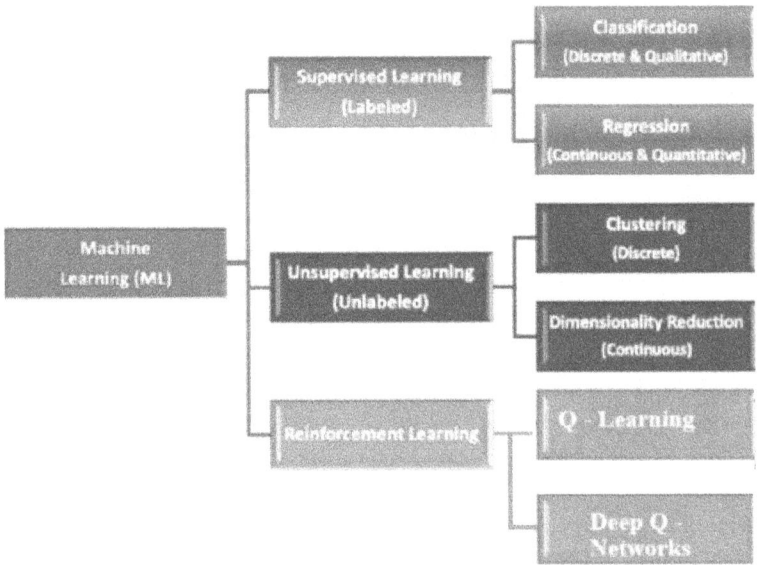

**Figure 1.1** Overview of machine learning techniques.

Machine learning (ML) includes a variety of methods and applications that are revolutionizing various fields, including engineering. These include predictive analytics to forecast future trends based on historical data, classification to assign items to predefined categories (Figure 1.1), clustering to group similar items, dimensionality reduction to minimize the number of variables considered, and reinforcement learning to train models that make sequential decisions that are desired through rewards. In engineering, ML techniques optimize processes, predict system behavior, and improve designs and decision-making, resulting in smarter, more efficient, and more adaptive systems [2].

The importance of ML in engineering is manifold. Improved predictive capabilities such as failure prediction allow for the prediction of equipment failures and the need for maintenance, reducing downtime and costs. Similarly, load forecasting allows for more accurate prediction of energy or material loads, optimizing resource allocation. Improved design and optimization are achieved through design automation, where ML optimizes design parameters to improve performance, cost-effectiveness, and material savings, and process optimization, where manufacturing processes are adjusted in real time to improve quality and efficiency. Additionally, ML facilitates data-driven insights through pattern recognition, which uncovers hidden patterns and correlations within large datasets, and anomaly detection, which identifies deviations from normal operations that may indicate potential problems [3].

Adaptive systems in engineering benefit from ML by developing adaptive control systems that learn and adapt to changing conditions and environments, as well as enabling autonomous systems such as robots and vehicles through reinforcement learning and other ML techniques. Additionally, ML improves operational efficiency by integrating predictive maintenance, optimizing supply chains, and improving energy management. This comprehensive integration of ML into engineering will address complex problems that are difficult or impossible to solve using traditional methods, significantly advancing the field and contributing to the development of innovative solutions [4].

## 1.2 Categories of Machine Learning

Machine learning techniques can be broadly categorized into three main types: Supervised Learning, Unsupervised Learning, and Reinforcement Learning.

### 1.2.1 Supervised Learning

Supervised learning is a fundamental branch of machine learning that trains models on labelled datasets to pair input data with the correct output. The main goal is to learn an input-to-output mapping that can be used to predict new, unknown data. The process begins with collecting a data set that contains input-output pairs. Each input is a set of features or variables, and each corresponding output is a target variable or label that the model is designed to predict. In supervised learning, a model is trained by iteratively adjusting parameters to minimize the difference between the prediction and the actual output. This tuning is typically achieved through an optimization algorithm such as gradient descent. The model's performance is evaluated using a separate validation set to ensure that the model generalizes well to new data and avoid overfitting, which occurs when a model learns the training data too closely to perform well on unknown data [5].

Supervised learning includes two main types of tasks: regression and classification. The goal of a regression task is to predict a continuous numeric value. Examples include predicting house prices based on characteristics such as location, size, and number of rooms, or predicting stock prices based on historical data. The goal of a classification task is to assign inputs to predefined categories or classes. For example, email spam detection classifies emails as spam or non-spam, and image recognition models classify images into categories such as cats, dogs, and cars.

There are many different algorithms available for implementing supervised learning, each with their own advantages and disadvantages. Linear and logistic regression are among the simplest methods and are used for regression and binary classification tasks, respectively. More complex algorithms include decision trees, which split data into subsets based on feature values, and support vector machines, which find the optimal hyperplane that separates different classes. Ensemble techniques, such as random forests and gradient boosting machines, combine multiple models to improve performance and robustness.

Neural networks, especially deep learning models, have gained prominence in supervised learning due to their ability to handle large data sets and complex patterns. These models consist of multiple layers of interconnected nodes or neurons that learn hierarchical representations of the input data. Deep learning has revolutionized fields such as computer vision, natural language processing, and speech recognition by achieving unprecedented levels of accuracy [6].

Despite its effectiveness, supervised learning requires large amounts of labeled data, which can be time-consuming and costly to acquire. Furthermore, the quality of the model depends heavily on the quality and diversity of the training data: improperly labeled or biased data can lead to inaccurate predictions and perpetuate existing biases. It includes a wide range of algorithms and techniques, from simple linear models to complex neural networks, and has applications in a wide range of domains, from finance and healthcare to marketing and technology. Its success depends on the availability of high-quality labeled data and careful evaluation to ensure robust and generalizable models.

### 1.2.2 Unsupervised Learning

Unsupervised learning is a type of machine learning that involves analyzing and modeling data without predefined labels or categories. Unlike supervised learning, where the model is trained on labelled data, unsupervised learning works with data that has no clear outcome, making it suitable for discovering patterns and structure hidden in Data. The main goal is to discover the underlying structure of the data, group similar data points, and identify important patterns or features [7].

The two main tasks of unsupervised learning are clustering and dimensionality reduction. Clustering involves grouping a set of objects in such a way that objects in the same group (or cluster) are more similar to each other than objects in other groups. One of the most popular clustering algorithms is k-means, which divides data into k clusters based on similar features. Another widely used algorithm is hierarchical clustering, which builds a tree of clusters by merging or splitting them multiple times. Clustering has many different applications, such as customer segmentation in marketing, social network analysis, and organizing large sets of documents.

On the other hand, dimensionality reduction aims to reduce the number of variables considered by creating a new, smaller set of variables that retains most of the important information from the original dataset. Principal component analysis (PCA) is a well-known technique in this genre. It transforms data into a set of orthogonal components, ordered according to the amount of variance they explain in the data. Another technique is distributed stochastic neighbour embedding (t-SNE), which is especially useful for visualizing high-dimensional data by mapping it into two or three dimensions. Dimensionality reduction is crucial for simplifying models, reducing computational costs, and alleviating the curse of dimensionality in data analysis [8].

Unsupervised learning also includes anomaly detection techniques, the goal of which is to identify data points that deviate significantly from the norm. This is valuable in areas such as fraud detection, cyber security and quality control. Algorithms such as isolated forests and Gaussian mixture models (GMM) are often used for this purpose. One of the strengths of unsupervised learning is the ability to work with unlabelled data, which is often more available and less expensive than labelled data. However, this also poses a challenge, as the lack of labelled examples means that evaluating the performance of unsupervised models can be more difficult. Validation often relies on subjective criteria or domain knowledge to interpret results.

Another challenge is the possibility of discovering patterns that are neither meaningful nor useful. Without explicit labels to guide the learning process, unsupervised learning algorithms can capture noisy or irrelevant structures in the data. Therefore, careful preprocessing and selection of appropriate techniques are important. Unsupervised learning is widely used in exploratory data analysis, where the goal is to understand the data and discover hidden structures. It is also applied to feature learning, where the model automatically learns useful features from raw data, which can then be used in other machine learning tasks. For example, auto encoders, a type of neural network used for unsupervised learning, can learn compressed representations of data, which can be used for tasks such as image de-noising and playback, appear abnormal [9].

It includes many different techniques such as clustering, dimensionality reduction, and anomaly detection, each with its own set of algorithms and applications. Despite its challenges, such as the difficulty of evaluating models and the risk of capturing irrelevant patterns, unsupervised learning plays an important role in exploratory data analysis, Characteristics and many practical applications in different fields.

### 1.2.3 Reinforcement Learning

Reinforcement learning (RL) is a type of machine learning in which an agent is trained to make a sequence of decisions by interacting with an environment in order to maximize a cumulative reward. Unlike supervised learning, in which a model learns from a dataset of labeled examples, in RL, the agent learns through trial and error by receiving feedback about its actions in the form of rewards or punishments. This feedback loop allows the agent to develop a policy, which is a strategy for choosing an action based on the current state of the environment [10].

The basic components of reinforcement learning are agent, environment, state, action, and reward. The agent is the learner or decision maker, and the environment is the external system with which the agent interacts. The agent constantly observes the state of the environment, chooses an action based on its policy, and receives a reward from the environment. The goal of the agent is to learn a policy that maximizes the total cumulative reward over time, called the return.

One of the main challenges of RL is the exploration-exploitation dilemma. The agent must find a balance between exploring the environment to discover new, potentially better actions, and exploiting its current knowledge to maximize rewards. Different strategies, such as epsilon greedy and High Confidence Bounds (UCB), are used to address this challenge by allowing the agent to fully explore for efficient learning while exploiting information. known information to receive high rewards.

Several algorithms have been developed for reinforcement learning, each with different approaches to learning optimal policies. Q-learning is a widely used model-free algorithm in which the agent learns a value function, called the Q function, that estimates the expected return of a particular action in a given state [11]. By updating Q values through repeated interactions with the environment, the agent gradually improves its policy. Another popular algorithm is Deep Q-Network (DQN), which combines Q-learning with deep neural networks to handle high-dimensional state spaces, such as those found in games. play game.

The policy gradient method is another type of RL algorithm that directly optimizes the policy by adjusting its parameters towards the gradient of the expected reward. These methods, including Proximal Policy Optimization (PPO) and Trusted Region Policy Optimization (TRPO), are particularly useful in the continuous action space and have been successfully applied in complex tasks such as robot control and autonomous driving (12).

Reinforcement learning has many applications in many different fields. In robotics, RL enables robots to learn complex behaviors and adapt to dynamic environments through self-directed exploration. In finance, RL is used to develop trading strategies that adapt to changing market conditions. RL also played an important role in the field of video gaming, where he achieved superhuman achievements in games such as Go, chess, and various other video games by learning strategies optimization through extensive simulation and interaction.

Despite its successes, reinforcement learning faces several challenges. A large number of interactions with the environment are often needed to learn effective policies, which can be computationally expensive and time-consuming. Additionally, RL algorithms can suffer from stability and convergence problems, especially in environments where rewards are rare or delayed. Researchers are actively investigating methods to improve the sample efficiency, stability, and generalization of RL algorithms to address these challenges [13].

By balancing exploration and exploitation and using algorithms such as Q-learning, political gradients, and their deep learning extensions, RL enables the development of intelligent agents capable of perform complex tasks. Its applications span a wide range of fields, from robotics and finance to gaming and autonomous systems, highlighting its potential to revolutionize industries through adaptive and autonomous decision making.

## 1.3 Algorithms

One of the most common algorithms in Supervised, Unsupervised and Reinforcement techniques are discussed.

### 1.3.1 Linear Regression Algorithm

Linear regression aims to establish a linear relationship between a dependent variable and one or more independent variables. It is often used in engineering for predictive modeling and trend analysis. The algorithm finds the best-fit line by minimizing the mean squared error [14] and [15].

1.  **Input:**
    Training data: $X=\{x_1,x_2,...,x_n\}$
    Target values: $Y=\{y_1,y_2,...,y_n\}$
2.  **Initialize:**
    Weights W (often starting with zero or random values)
    Bias b (often starting with zero)
3.  **Hypothesis:**
    h(x)=W·x+b
4.  **Cost Function (Mean Squared Error):**

$$J(W,b) = (\frac{1}{2m}) \sum_{i=1}^{m} (h(x_i) - y_i)^2$$

5.  **Gradient Descent:**
    Repeat until convergence:
    Update weights: $W = W - \alpha \frac{\partial J(W,b)}{\partial W}$
    Update bias: $b = b - \alpha \frac{\partial J(W,b)}{\partial b}$
    Where $\alpha$ is the learning rate.
6.  **Output:**
    Trained weights W and bias b.

In Figure 1.2, visualization of linear regression output is shown.

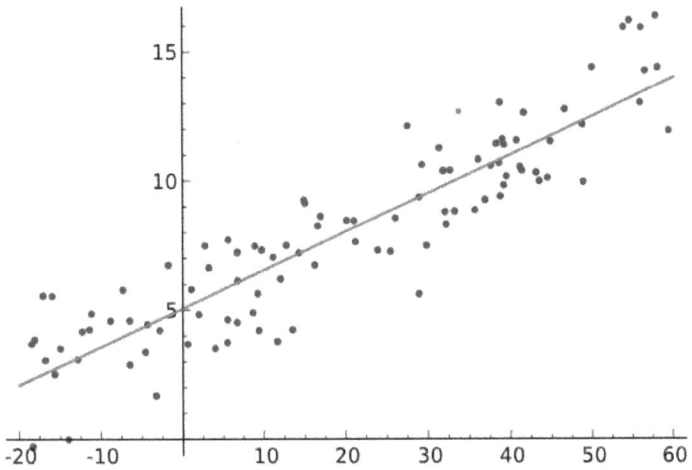

**Figure 1.2** Linear regression visualization.

### 1.3.2 K-Means Clustering Algorithm:

K-Means clustering is an unsupervised learning algorithm used to partition data into kkk clusters. Each cluster is represented by its centroid and data points are assigned to the closest centroid. This method is useful for pattern recognition and anomaly detection in technical data [16] and [17].

1. **Input:**
   Data points: X={x1,x2,...,xn}
   Number of clusters: k
2. **Initialize:**
   Randomly select k data points as initial centroids: μ1,μ2,...,μk
3. **Assign Clusters:**
   For each data point xi:
   Assign xi to the cluster with the nearest centroid:
   Cj={xi:‖xi−μj‖≤‖xi−μl‖∀l,1≤l≤k}
4. **Update Centroids:**
   For each cluster j:
   Update centroid μj: $\mu_j = \frac{1}{|C_j|}\sum_{x_i \in C_j} x_i$
5. **Repeat:**

Repeat the Assign Clusters and Update Centroids steps until Centroids do not change significantly. Iteration result is shown in Figure 1.3.

6. **Output:**
   Final cluster assignments and centroids.

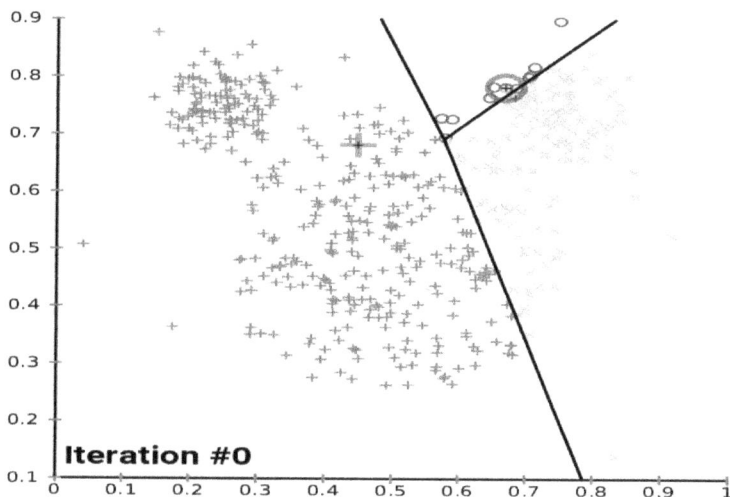

**Figure 1.3** K-Means clustering process.

### 1.3.3 Q-Learning Algorithm:

Q-Learning is a model-free reinforcement learning algorithm that aims to learn the value of performing a certain action in a certain state. It is especially useful in the field of robotics and adaptive control systems in engineering. The agent interacts with the environment, updates the Q value based on the reward, and aims to maximize the cumulative reward over time [18].

1. **Initialize:**
   Q-table with zeros: $Q(s,a)=0 \forall s \in S, a \in A$
   Learning rate $\alpha$
   Discount factor $\gamma$
   Exploration rate $\epsilon$
2. **Repeat (for each episode):**
   Initialize state s

Repeat (for each step of the episode):
Choose action a using policy derived from Q (e.g., ε-greedy)
Take action a, observe reward r and next state s′
Update Q-value: $Q(s,a)=Q(s,a)+\alpha[r+\gamma\max_{a'}Q(s',a')-Q(s,a)]$
Update state s=s′
If s is terminal, end the episode.
   3.   **Output:** Optimized Q-table for action selection

## 1.4. Comparison of Techniques and Algorithms

Table 1.1 presents a comparison between different types of machine learning. This comparative summary provides a high-level overview of the key differences, advantages, and disadvantages of supervised, unsupervised, and reinforcement learning techniques, as well as applications.

**Table 1.1** Comparison of supervised, unsupervised, and reinforcement Learning

| Aspect | Supervised Learning | Unsupervised Learning | Reinforcement Learning |
|---|---|---|---|
| Data | Labeled data | Unlabeled data | Interactions with the environment |
| Goal | Predict outputs from inputs | Discover patterns/structures in data | Maximize cumulative reward |
| Techniques | Classification, Regression | Clustering, Dimensionality Reduction | Q-learning, Policy Gradients |
| Advantages | High accuracy, easy to implement | Works with unlabeled data, reveals hidden patterns | Adaptation, suitable for dynamic environments |

| Disad-vantages | Requires labeled data, risk of overfitting | Hard to evaluate, might find irrelevant patterns | High computational cost, needs many interactions |
|---|---|---|---|
| Applications | Image recognition, Medical diagnosis, Spam detection | Customer segmentation, Anomaly detection, Market analysis | Game playing, Robotics, Autonomous driving |

Table 1.2 summarizes the main characteristics of the Linear Regression, K-Means Clustering, and Q-Learning algorithm types, highlighting their differences in learning approaches, areas of application, advantages and disadvantages.

**Table 1.2** Comparison of linear regression, K-means clustering, and Q-learning algorithms

| Aspect | Linear Regression | K-means Clustering | Q-learning |
|---|---|---|---|
| Type of Learning | Supervised | Unsupervised | Reinforcement |
| Objective | Predict continuous output | Cluster data points | Maximize cumulative reward |
| Input Data | Labeled (input, output pairs) | Unlabeled (data points) | State, Action, Reward |
| Output | Continuous values (predictions) | Cluster centroids or memberships | Action decisions based on policy |

| | | | |
|---|---|---|---|
| Training Approach | Minimize error between predictions and actual outputs | Minimize variance within clusters | Learn optimal policy through trial and error |
| Evaluation | RMSE, R-squared | Silhouette score, Inertia | Cumulative reward, Value function |
| Application | Prediction tasks (e.g., sales forecasting) | Customer segmentation, Image compression | Game playing (e.g., AlphaGo), Robotics |
| Algorithm Examples | Ordinary Least Squares, Ridge Regression | Lloyd's Algorithm, Elkan's Algorithm | Q-learning, SARSA, Deep Q-Networks |
| Advantages | Simple, interpretable | Finds natural groupings in data | Learns from interaction with environment |
| Disadvantages | Assumes linear relationship, sensitive to outliers | Requires predefined number of clusters, sensitive to initialization | Requires exploration-exploitation balance |

## 1.5 Conclusion

Explore supervised, unsupervised, and reinforcement learning techniques as well as specific algorithms such as linear regression, k-means clustering, and Q-learning that reveal the breadth and depth of possibilities that Machine learning brings in different fields of engineering. These methodologies empower engineers with powerful tools to predict outcomes, uncover hidden patterns, and optimize decision-making processes.

The hallmark of supervised learning is the ability to predict outcomes with high accuracy. Labelled data is used to train a model that transfers appropriately to new inputs. Techniques such as linear regression provide interpretable results and are particularly useful in scenarios where understanding the relationships between variables is important, such as predictive maintenance and system optimization.

Unsupervised learning plays a crucial role in engineering by uncovering hidden patterns and structures within data that might not be apparent through manual analysis. K-means clustering, for instance, enables engineers to segment data into meaningful groups, facilitating tasks like anomaly detection and resource allocation optimization.

Reinforcement learning is more complex to implement, but offers significant advantages in adaptive control and decision-making. Algorithms such as Q-learning enable automated systems to learn optimal behaviors through trial and error, making them suitable for applications in robotics, autonomous vehicles, and process optimization where the environment is Dynamics require continuous learning and optimization.

In the realm of advanced engineering solutions, the integration of these machine learning techniques has revolutionized traditional approaches by offering smarter, data-driven insights and optimizations. Linear regression aids in precise predictive modeling, k-means clustering enhances understanding of complex datasets, and Q-learning enables systems to autonomously improve their performance over time. Together, these methodologies contribute to more efficient designs, enhanced predictive capabilities, and adaptive systems that respond dynamically to changing conditions.

As machine learning continues to evolve, its application in engineering promises to further advance, solving increasingly complex problems and pushing the boundaries of what is achievable in optimizing processes, predicting system behaviors, and enabling autonomous decision-making across various engineering disciplines. By embracing these techniques, engineers can leverage data-driven insights to innovate and excel in the face of modern challenges.

# References

[1] Goodfellow, I., Bengio, Y., & Courville, A. (2016). Deep Learning. MIT Press.

[2] Murphy, K. P. (2012). Machine Learning: A Probabilistic Perspective. MIT Press.

[3] Blei, D. M., Ng, A. Y., & Jordan, M. I. (2003). "Latent Dirichlet Allocation." Journal of Machine Learning Research 3, 993-1022.

[4] LeCun, Y., Bengio, Y., & Hinton, G. (2015). "Deep Learning." Nature 521 (7553), 436-444.

[5] Domingos, Pedro. "A Few Useful Things to Know About Machine Learning." Communications of the ACM 55, no. 10 (2012): 78-87.

[6] Hastie, Trevor, Robert Tibshirani, and Jerome Friedman. The Elements of Statistical Learning: Data Mining, Inference, and Prediction. New York: Springer, 2009.

[7] Bishop, Christopher M. *Pattern Recognition and Machine Learning.* New York: Springer, 2006.

[8] Han, Jiawei, Micheline Kamber, and Jian Pei. Data Mining: Concepts and Techniques. 3rd ed. Waltham: Morgan Kaufmann, 2011.

[9] Guyon, Isabelle, and André Elisseeff. "An Introduction to Variable and Feature Selection." Journal of Machine Learning Research 3 (2003): 1157-1182.

[10] Sutton, Richard S., and Andrew G. Barto. *Reinforcement Learning: An Introduction.* 2nd ed. Cambridge: MIT Press, 2018.

[11] Szepesvári, Csaba. Algorithms for Reinforcement Learning. Synthesis Lectures on Artificial Intelligence and Machine Learning. San Rafael: Morgan & Claypool, 2010.

[12] Mnih, Volodymyr, Koray Kavukcuoglu, David Silver, Andrei A. Rusu, Joel Veness, Marc G. Bellemare, Alex Graves, et al. "Playing Atari with Deep Reinforcement Learning." *arXiv preprint arXiv:1312.5602* (2013).

[13] Schulman, John, Sergey Levine, Pieter Abbeel, Michael Jordan, and Philipp Moritz. "Trust Region Policy Optimization." In Proceedings of the 32nd International Conference on Machine Learning (ICML), 1889-1897. 2015.

[14] Seber, George A. F., and Alan J. Lee. Linear Regression Analysis. 2nd ed. Hoboken, NJ: John Wiley & Sons, 2003.

[15] Draper, Norman R., and Harry Smith. Applied Regression Analysis. 3rd ed. Hoboken, NJ: John Wiley & Sons, 1998.

[16] MacQueen, J. B. "Some Methods for Classification and Analysis of Multivariate Observations." In Proceedings of the Fifth Berkeley

Symposium on Mathematical Statistics and Probability, Volume 1: Statistics, 281-297. Berkeley, CA: University of California Press, 1967.

[17] Lloyd, Stuart P. "Least Squares Quantization in PCM." IEEE Transactions on Information Theory 28, no. 2 (1982): 129-137.

[18] Watkins, Christopher J. C. H., and Peter Dayan. "Q-learning." Machine Learning 8, no. 3-4 (1992): 279-292.

# Chapter 2

## AI-Powered Crop Prediction for Sustainable Agriculture

**S. Mohana, Fariya Rahmath, Gayathri Devy S, Janani Shanmugi M A and Chaarubhala S**
Dept of CSE, Saranathan College of Engineering, Tamil Nadu, India

## Abstract

Agriculture plays a critical role in sustaining the global population, but it faces growing challenges due to climate variability, inefficient resource use, and outdated farming practices. Traditional crop prediction methods often fail to account for the complex interplay between weather, soil conditions, and crop characteristics. The advent of machine learning (ML) and artificial intelligence (AI) offers new opportunities to enhance agricultural productivity by leveraging large datasets and advanced prediction models. This project introduces an AI-powered crop prediction system, "SmartFarm," designed to assist farmers in making informed decisions on crop selection, planting, and harvesting. By integrating weather and geolocation data through APIs, the system delivers real-time, location-specific insights, optimizing the yield and sustainability of agricultural operations. The user-friendly interface ensures that farmers can access and apply these insights easily, leading to more efficient farming practices and improved profitability.

**Keywords:** Artificial Intelligence (AI), Machine Learning (ML), Yield Prediction, Sustainable Agriculture.

## 2.1 Introduction

Traditional farming methods often rely on generational knowledge and experience, but they can struggle to adapt to rapidly changing environmental factors such as erratic rainfall, extreme temperatures, and fluctuating soil quality. Inaccurate or uninformed crop selection and poor timing of planting or harvesting can lead to low yields, increased susceptibility to pests, and a higher dependency on chemical fertilizers and pesticides. This, in turn, contributes to environmental degradation and economic losses for farmers.

Moreover, the effects of climate change are becoming more pronounced, with increasingly frequent droughts, floods, and unseasonal rains. Farmers need to make timely, data-driven decisions to mitigate the risks associated with such uncertainties. However, access to reliable, real-time information about weather conditions, soil health, and market demands remains limited, particularly in rural and remote areas.

AI offers a powerful solution to many of these challenges by enabling more accurate predictions and data-driven decision-making in agriculture. Machine learning models can analyze vast amounts of data, identifying patterns and correlations that may not be immediately apparent to human decision-makers.

By integrating weather forecasts, geolocation data, and soil characteristics, AI-powered systems can offer tailored recommendations to farmers, helping them choose the right crops, optimal planting and harvesting times, and efficient resource utilization strategies. With AI, farmers can predict crop outcomes more accurately, avoid resource wastage, and implement sustainable agricultural practices that reduce soil degradation and water usage.

By integrating AI into crop prediction, farmers can now anticipate how different variables—such as rainfall, temperature, soil moisture, and nutrient levels—will affect crop growth and productivity. Machine learning algorithms can analyze these complex datasets and offer real-time recommendations on the best times to plant, irrigate, fertilize, and harvest. Furthermore, AI models are adaptive, continuously learning from new data to refine their predictions and respond to changing conditions like climate variability or pest outbreaks.

## 2.2 Related Work

Crop yield prediction is an essential task for the decision-makers at national and regional levels (e.g., the EU level) for rapid decision-making. An accurate crop yield prediction model can help farmers to decide on what to grow and when to grow. There are different approaches to crop yield prediction. This review article has investigated what has been done on the use of machine learning in crop yield prediction in the literature. During our analysis of the retrieved publications, one of the exclusion criteria is that the publication is a survey

20

or traditional review paper. Those excluded publications are, in fact, related work and are discussed in this section. Chlingaryan and Suk-karieh performed a review study on nitrogen status estimation using machine learning (Chlingaryan et al., 2018). The paper concludes that quick developments in sensing technologies and ML techniques will result in cost-effective solutions in the agricultural sector.

Elavarasan et al. performed a survey of publications on machine learning models associated with crop yield prediction based on climatic parameters. The paper advises looking broad to find more parameters that account for crop yield (Elavarasan et al., 2018). Liakos et al. (2018) published a review paper on the application of machine learning in the agricultural sector. The analysis was performed with publications focusing on crop management, livestock management, water management, and soil management. Li, Lecourt, and Bishop performed a review study on determining the ripeness of fruits to decide the optimal harvest time and yield prediction (Li et al., 2018). Mayuri and Priya addressed the challenges and methodologies that are encountered in the field of image processing and machine learning in the agricultural sector and especially in the detection of diseases (Mayuri and Priya). Somvanshi and Mishra presented several machine learning approaches and their application in plant biology (Somvanshi and Mishra, 2015). Gandhi and Armstrong published a review paper on the application of data mining in the agricultural sector in general, dealing with decision making. They concluded that further research needs to be done to see how the implementation of data mining into complex agricultural datasets could be realized (Gandhi and Armstrong, 2016).

Machine learning (ML) has emerged as a powerful tool in agriculture, enabling predictive models that analyze large datasets for improving farming practices. Studies by Kamilaris et al. (2018) highlight the use of ML in yield prediction, disease detection, and crop classification. Common algorithms like Decision Trees, Random Forests, and Neural Networks are widely employed for crop prediction due to their accuracy in analyzing weather and soil data (Gandhi et al., 2016).

ML-driven crop prediction models contribute to better resource management, reduced waste, and enhanced crop yields, making agriculture more efficient and environmentally friendly. Past research indicates the efficacy of AI and machine learning models in agriculture. Studies have explored the use of AI for soil quality analysis, weather prediction, and crop yield estimation. However, few systems provide a holistic approach that integrates multiple data sources (weather, soil, and geolocation) for real-time decision-making.

**AI for crop yield prediction:** Previous works have used machine learning algorithms like Random Forest, SVM, and neural networks to predict crop yields based on historical data. Studies show that Random Forest (RF) models are particularly effective in handling large datasets with multiple variables, making them suitable for crop yield prediction. For instance, a study by Lobell et al. (2015) demonstrated that RF can accurately predict wheat and maize yields based on environmental variables like temperature and soil moisture.

**Weather and climate models:** Research shows that weather data combined with AI can significantly improve prediction accuracy for agricultural purposes. Systems like WeatherStack and OpenWeatherMap provide real-time data through APIs, which can be integrated into crop prediction models to enhance accuracy. Gopalakrishnan et al. (2021) explored the use of these APIs to adjust farming schedules based on current weather conditions, resulting in improved yields.

**Geolocation and soil quality analysis:** Combining soil properties with geographical data allows for better crop recommendations. Ramesh et al. (2020) demonstrated that combining soil data with machine learning models improved the accuracy of crop yield predictions. Their study showed that soil pH, moisture, and organic content are strong predictors of crop performance. Geospatial data collected through GPS or satellite imagery helps in assessing land suitability for different crops.

Sustainable agriculture is becoming increasingly critical as the global population rises and climate change exacerbates the challenges of food security. Farmers and agricultural stakeholders must not only optimize crop yields but also ensure the sustainability of farming practices to preserve the environment and resources for future generations. Traditional farming methods, which heavily rely on manual observations and past experiences, often fail to adapt to dynamic environmental conditions such as fluctuating weather patterns, soil degradation, and pest infestations.

In this context, technological innovations like artificial intelligence (AI) are emerging as powerful tools for transforming agriculture. AI-powered crop prediction systems can revolutionize farming by providing accurate, data-driven insights that help farmers make informed decisions. These systems leverage vast amounts of data from various sources such as satellite imagery, soil sensors, climate models, and historical crop data to predict crop yields, optimize resource use, and reduce the environmental impact of farming operations.

Sparrow et al. provided proper strategies may be needed when AI begins to affect the agriculture sector. The study pointed out some of the consequences which may arise due to the implementation of AI technology in agriculture sector. According to the authors, AI may be beneficial for farmers, end users and the environment but may present unknown risks and suggested some alternative designs and regulatory procedures have been suggested to the risks. The civil and principled impacts of using AI in the farming were studied to find out how are they correlated with AI ethics based on sustainability, trust, privacy, benefits, transparency, freedom, responsibility, justice, morality, and unanimity.

Vincent et al. mentioned that currently some of the farmers are using automated equipment fed through huge data collected by meteorological sensors and satellite imagery. These farmers act in accordance with the advice provided by sophisticated computer applications. Existing investment on precision agriculture assures an important role of AI in agriculture. The ML methods are expected to address key research topics in agriculture sector, which include meteorological parameter prediction ahead of time, economic modelling, and plant and animal breeding. Furthermore, AI and ML methods have the potential to improve distribution, balance energy consumption loads, and manage fluctuations in renewable energy production. The energy transition can incorporate AI into their system for more opportunities to improve the efficiency of production and consumption.

For the development of the precise and sustainable agriculture sector development, nanotechnology can offer excellent opportunities, discussed in review articles covering strategies to improve crop nutrition and develop smart plant sensors. Nanotechnology can facilitate the delivery of fertilisers to tissues and organisms in a controlled way, which would be beneficial for plant growth and optimal use of fertilizers and pesticides and minimise adverse effect on soil condition. Furthermore, nanotechnology applications in agriculture include the plant sensor development through which the plants can itself sense abiotic stress depending on the directed delivery of nanomaterials. Four main areas in which nanotechnology is progressing include improving production yield, soil conditions, and efficiency of materials usage.

Additionally, the integration of nanotechnologies with AI-driven methodologies amplifies these advancements in agriculture. AI complements nanotechnologies by providing intelligent data analysis, predictive modelling, and autonomous decision-making capabilities. The fusion of nanotechnology and AI promises novel opportunities in precision farming, allowing for real-time monitoring, precise resource management, and informed decision support systems. This collaboration aims to revolutionize agricultural practices, enhancing productivity, sustainability, and efficiency in the face of global agricultural challenges.

The Indian Council of Agricultural Research (ICAR) has implemented a drone-based crop monitoring system powered by AI algorithms. This system uses high-resolution imagery captured by drones to assess crop health, detect stress factors, and identify pest infestations. In a pilot project conducted in the state of Uttar Pradesh, ICAR's AI system was able to detect and map areas affected by the fall armyworm pest, a significant threat to maize crops. This early detection allowed for targeted interventions, minimizing crop losses and maximizing yields (ICAR, 2022).

The Center for Irrigation Technology at California State University, Fresno, has developed an AI-based irrigation management system called "WISE" (Water Irrigation Suggestion Engine). This system integrates data from soil moisture sensors, weather stations, and crop water demand models to provide real-time irrigation recommendations tailored to individual fields and crop types. In a case study conducted on almond orchards in the San Joaquin Valley, the WISE system achieved water savings of up to 20% while maintaining or improving crop yields. The system's ability to optimize irrigation scheduling and prevent over-watering not only conserved water resources but also reduced energy costs associated with pumping and distributing water (Centre for Irrigation Technology, 2020).

The Queensland Alliance for Agriculture and Food Innovation (QAAFI) at the University of Queensland has implemented an AI-powered crop phenotyping platform to accelerate the breeding of improved wheat varieties. This platform uses computer vision and machine learning algorithms to analyze high-throughput phenotypic data collected from field trials and identify desirable traits, such as drought tolerance and disease resistance. In a case study focused on drought-tolerant wheat breeding, QAAFI's AI system was able to accurately identify and select wheat lines with superior drought tolerance based on their phenotypic characteristics. This accelerated the breeding process and facilitated the development of drought-tolerant wheat varieties suitable for Australian growing conditions (QAAFI, 2019).

Canada (AAFC) has developed an AI-based system for weed detection and management in field crops. This system uses deep learning algorithms to analyze high-resolution imagery captured by drones or ground-based sensors, accurately identifying and classifying weed species present in the field. In a case study conducted on canola fields in Saskatchewan, AAFC's AI system was able to detect and map the presence of various weed species, such as wild mustard, wild oats, and green foxtail, with an accuracy of over 90%. This information enabled targeted herbicide applications, reducing the need for blanket spraying and promoting sustainable weed management practices (AAFC, 2023).

## 2.3 Proposed System

The proposed AI-Powered Crop Prediction for Sustainable Agriculture system leverages a Deep Neural Network (DNN) to help farmers make informed decisions about crop selection and yield prediction. The system integrates real-time data from various sources, including weather, soil conditions, geolocation, and historical crop yields.

After collecting and preprocessing this data, the DNN model analyses complex patterns and relationships among the factors that influence crop performance.

The system aims to provide precise recommendations by predicting the most suitable crops for specific conditions or estimating the potential yield for a particular season. It can be deployed through a web or mobile interface, allowing farmers to input their data and receive crop recommendations tailored to their geographic and environmental conditions. This intelligent, data-driven approach supports sustainable agriculture by optimizing crop selection and helping farmers plan better, reduce risk, and increase productivity.

### 2.3.1Proposed System Architecture

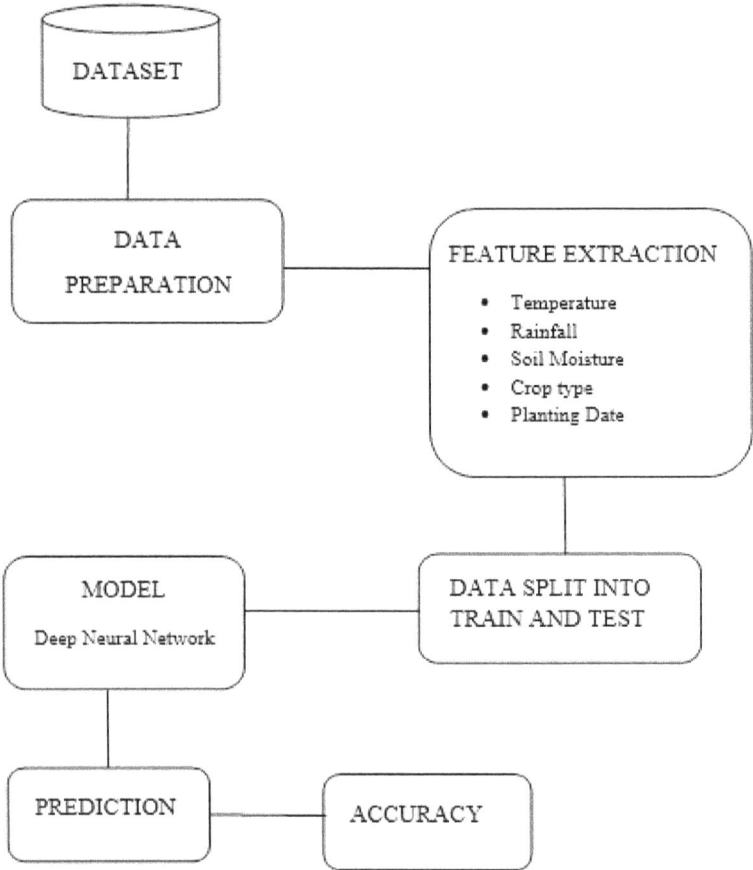

**Figure 2.1** AI-powered crop prediction system architecture.

## 2.3.2 Proposed System Working

### Dataset

A group of data points that a computer can use for analysis and prediction as a single entity.

### Data Preprocessing

Data preprocessing is a crucial step in machine learning projects, ensuring that the data is clean, consistent, and suitable for model training. For crop prediction, this involves handling missing values, outliers, and inconsistencies in historical crop and weather data. Normalization or standardization of numerical features is essential to prevent features with larger magnitudes from dominating the learning process. Categorical features like crop type and soil type should be converted into numerical representations using techniques like one-hot encoding or label encoding. Feature engineering can create new informative features by combining existing ones, such as calculating growing season length or average temperature during specific growth stages. If the dataset is imbalanced, techniques like over-sampling or under-sampling can help balance the classes. By carefully preprocessing the data, you can improve the accuracy and reliability of your crop prediction model.

### Feature Engineering

Combine multiple input features (like weather, soil, and location data) to create more meaningful attributes. For example, use rainfall and temperature to create an index for drought prediction. Incorporate time-based features like seasons, growing cycles, and weather forecasts for upcoming months. Add historical data trends as features to understand patterns in previous yields or weather conditions.

### Deep Neural Network Model

A Deep Neural Network (DNN) is a powerful machine learning algorithm that consists of multiple layers of neurons or nodes, allowing it to learn and model complex patterns in data. For an AI-powered crop prediction system in the context of sustainable agriculture, a DNN can be highly effective because it can model the intricate relationships between various factors such as weather, soil properties, crop types, and environmental conditions, leading to accurate predictions.

Input Layer: Input all the engineered features, such as weather, soil, geolocation, and historical data.
Hidden Layers: Multiple hidden layers are used with Rectified Linear Unit (ReLU) as the activation function. Implement dropout layers to prevent overfitting, especially in small datasets. Consider 2–4 dense hidden layers with 64, 128, or 256 neurons to start. Adjust based on the complexity of your dataset.

Output Layer: A linear output function for regression is used (yield as a continuous number).

Architecture: Input Layer: (weather, soil, geolocation, historical data)
    Hidden Layer 1: Dense (128 neurons, activation='ReLU')
    Dropout Layer: (Dropout rate=0.3)
    Hidden Layer 2: Dense (64 neurons, activation='ReLU')
    Dropout Layer: (Dropout rate=0.3)
    Output Layer: (softmax for classification / linear for regression)

**Training the model**

Loss Function: Categorical Crossentropy for crop-type classification. Mean Squared Error (MSE) for crop-yield prediction (regression).
Optimizer: Adam optimizer is used for faster convergence.

Evaluation Metric: Metrics like accuracy, precision, and recall are used for classification. Metrics like $R^2$ score, Mean Absolute Error (MAE), or Root Mean Squared Error (RMSE) are used for regression. Training Strategy: Techniques like early stopping are used to avoid overfitting.

**Post-Processing and Prediction Layer**

The model outputs either the most suitable crop type or the expected yield based on the input features.

The system predicts the crop yield based on current weather patterns, soil conditions, and crop history. By predicting how much water or fertilizer is needed, the DNN helps farmers optimize resource use, promoting sustainability by reducing waste.

**Deployment Layer**

The trained DNN model is deployed using TensorFlow Serving.

**Algorithm for predicting crop yield**

Input: Dataset containing the data of soil properties, weather, crop types and geolocation.
Output: Predicting crop yield or recommending crops
# Define DNN Model Architecture
    INPUT layer with shape (number_of_features)
    # Hidden Layers
    ADD dense layer with 128 neurons, activation 'ReLU'
    ADD dropout layer with rate 0.2
    ADD dense layer with 256 neurons, activation 'ReLU'
    ADD dropout layer with rate 0.2
    ADD dense layer with 128 neurons, activation 'ReLU'
    ADD dropout layer with rate 0.2
    # Output Layers
    ADD output layer for crop yield prediction with 1 neuron (linear activation)
    ADD output layer for crop recommendation with num_crops neurons (softmax activation)
  # Compile the Model
    - Optimizer: Adam
    - Loss function:
      - 'Mean Squared Error' for yield prediction
      - 'Categorical Cross-Entropy' for crop recommendation
    - Metrics:
      - 'Mean Squared Error' for yield
      - 'Accuracy' for crop recommendation
  # Train the Model
    - Input features (X_train)
    - Targets: y_train_yield (for crop yield), y_train_crop (for crop recommendation)
    - Validation data: (X_val, y_val_yield, y_val_crop)

- Epochs: 100
- Batch size: 32
# Evaluate the Model
EVALUATE the model on test data (X_test, y_test_yield, y_test_crop)
PRINT test loss, MSE for crop yield, and accuracy for crop recommendation
# Make Predictions
INPUT new data (weather_data_new, soil_data_new, etc.)
  predicted_yield = model.predict(new_data)[0]  # Yield Prediction
  predicted_crop = model.predict(new_data)[1]  # Crop Recommendation
  recommended_crop = argmax(predicted_crop)    # Select the best crop
PRINT predicted yield and recommended crop

## 2.4 Results and Visualizations

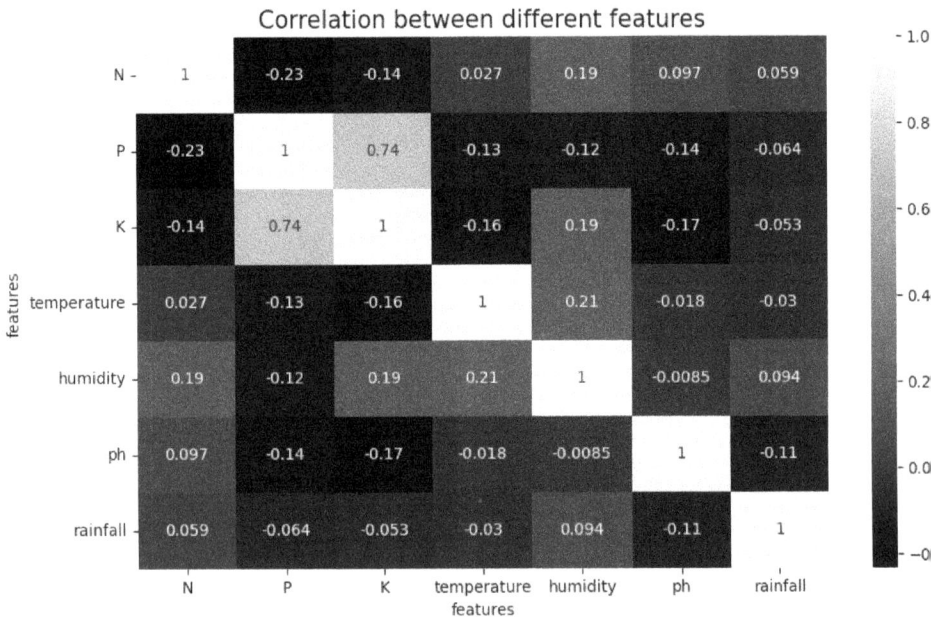

**Figure 2.2** Correlation between different features.

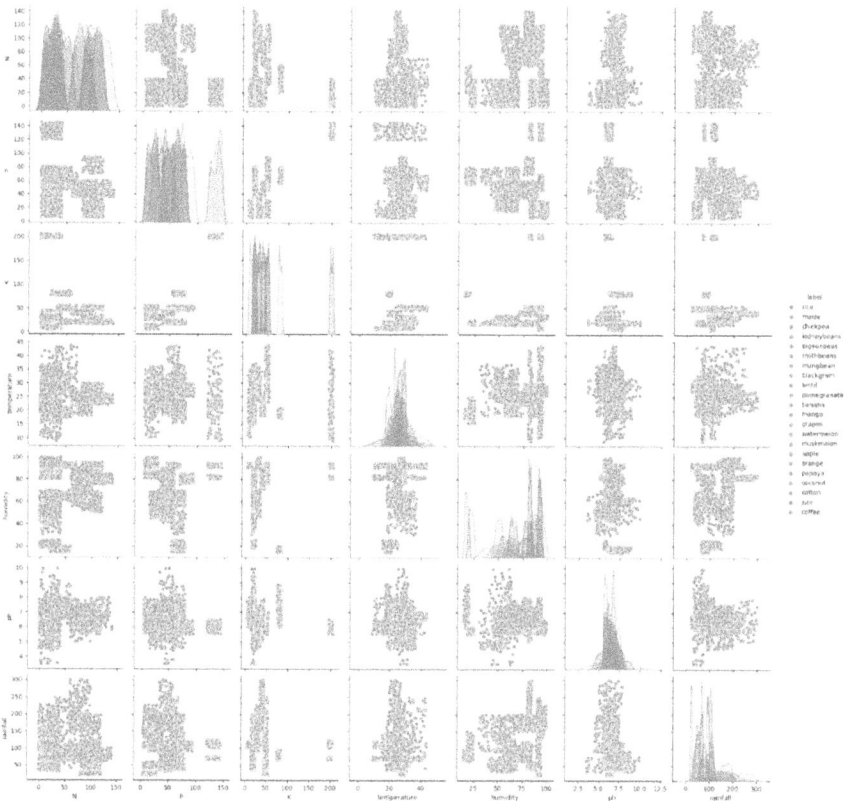

**Figure 2.3** Pairwise correlation plots for the features

## Conclusion

In conclusion, existing literature highlights the potential of integrating machine learning with real-time data from weather, soil, and geolocation APIs for crop prediction. However, few systems provide a comprehensive approach that combines all these factors in a user-friendly interface specifically designed for small-scale farmers. A Deep Neural Network is an advanced machine learning algorithm that can significantly enhance crop prediction systems by leveraging vast amounts of data to model complex relationships between environmental factors and crop outcomes. For sustainable agriculture, a DNN can predict yields, optimize resource usage, and improve decision-making for farmers, leading to increased productivity and

31

reduced environmental impact. Ultimately, this project represents a critical step toward empowering farmers with the knowledge and tools needed to practice smart, sustainable agriculture, ensuring long-term profitability and ecological balance. The future scopes include Integration with IoT devices for real-time soil monitoring and Expansion to include predictive pest and disease outbreak alerts based on climatic conditions.

## References

1. Gupta, Deependra Kumar, Anselmo Pagani, Paolo Zamboni, and Ajay Kumar Singh. "AI-powered revolution in plant sciences: advancements, applications, and challenges for sustainable agriculture and food security." *Exploration of Foods and Foodomics* 2, no. 5 (2024): 443-459.
2. Mana, A. A., A. Allouhi, A. Hamrani, S. Rahman, I. el Jamaoui, and K. Jayachandran. "Sustainable AI-Based Production Agriculture: Exploring AI Applications and Implications in Agricultural Practices." *Smart Agricultural Technology* (2024): 100416.
3. Gul, Danish, and Rizwan Ul Zama Banday. "Transforming Crop Management Through Advanced AI and Machine Learning: Insights into Innovative Strategies for Sustainable Agriculture." *AI, Computer Science and Robotics Technology* (2024).
4. Ashraf, Hadeed, and Musliudeen Toheeb Akanbi. "Sustainable Agriculture in the Digital Age: Crop Management and Yield Forecasting with IoT, Cloud, and AI." *Tensorgate Journal of Sustainable Technology and Infrastructure for Developing Countries* 6, no. 1 (2023): 64-71.

# Chapter 3

## Facial Expression Recognition Using Convolutional Neural Network

**R. Senthamil Selvi, P. Naveen and S. Naga Sharavanesh**
Department of Computer Science and Engineering, Saranathan College of Engineering, Panjappur, Trichy, Tamil Nadu, India

### Abstract

Facial expression recognition is an essential technology used in a variety of applications such as human-computer interaction, psychological analysis, and security systems. In this study, we propose a Convolutional Neural Network (CNN)-based approach to classify facial expressions into seven distinct categories: **angry, disgust, fear, happy, neutral, sad,** and **surprise**. Leveraging a deep learning model trained on the **Facial Expression Recognition (FER)** dataset, the approach integrates transfer learning and data augmentation to improve classification accuracy. Results show that the model achieved a notable accuracy of over 90% in detecting certain expressions, with CNN architecture effectively capturing complex facial features.

**Keywords:** Deep Learning, Convolutional Neural Networks, Transfer Learning, Facial Expression Recognition, Image Classification, FER Dataset

### 3.1 Introduction

Facial expression recognition (FER) plays a critical role in understanding human emotions, which has a wide range of practical applications, including automated customer feedback systems, surveillance, mental health monitoring, and human-computer interactions. Traditional image processing techniques struggle to effectively handle the subtleties and complexities of facial expressions in real-time settings. Recent advances in **deep learning**, particularly **Convolutional Neural Networks (CNNs)**, have revolutionized the ability to automatically extract meaningful features from facial images. CNNs are particularly suited for facial expression recognition due to their ability to capture spatial hierarchies in images. The model's architecture allows it to identify subtle differences in pixel intensity and position, making it highly effective for classifying facial expressions. This study proposes a deep CNN architecture that integrates transfer learning to enhance the accuracy of facial expression recognition, leveraging a large labeled dataset.

## 3.2 Related Work

Facial expression recognition has been a topic of interest in computer vision for years. Early methods primarily relied on handcrafted feature extraction, such as **Gabor filters** or **Histograms of Oriented Gradients (HOG)**. These approaches, while effective for small datasets, performed poorly when scaled or applied to complex real-world data.

With the advent of deep learning, CNNs have become the dominant method for FER. Studies such as [1] have employed models like **ResNet** and **InceptionV3**, showing substantial improvements in accuracy over traditional approaches. **Transfer learning** using a model pre-trained on a large dataset (like ImageNet) and fine-tuning it for a smaller, specific task has been particularly beneficial in overcoming the challenge of limited labeled data.

However, most previous studies faced challenges when it came to real-time performance or handling highly imbalanced datasets. This study addresses these issues by integrating transfer learning, data augmentation, and optimization techniques to achieve high accuracy while maintaining real-time feasibility.

## 3.3 Dataset and Preprocessing

### 3.3.1 Dataset

The **Facial Expression Recognition (FER) Dataset** used in this study comprises grayscale images of faces labeled with one of seven expressions: **angry, disgust, fear, happy, neutral, sad,** and **surprise**. The dataset contains **48x48 pixel images**, a resolution suitable for real-time processing. Each image has been preprocessed to remove any noise and standardize the pixel values.

### 3.3.2 Data Augmentation

To improve the generalization of the model, **data augmentation** techniques such as random **flipping, rotation, zooming, and shifting** were applied. These techniques increase the diversity of the training data, helping the model avoid overfitting and enhancing its ability to recognize expressions in varied scenarios.

### 3.3.3 Preprocessing Techniques

- **Normalization**: Pixel values were normalized to fall within the range [0, 1] to accelerate training and improve model convergence.
- **Label Encoding**: The categorical labels (expressions) were encoded using **one-hot encoding** to represent the seven classes as binary vectors.

### 3.4 Proposed Model

### 3.4.1 Convolutional Neural Network Architecture

The proposed model is based on a **Convolutional Neural Network (CNN)** architecture, which includes multiple layers for feature extraction and classification:

- o **Convolutional Layers**: These layers are responsible for extracting local features such as edges, textures, and patterns from the input images.
- o **Max Pooling Layers**: These layers reduce the dimensionality of the feature maps, thereby reducing the computational complexity of the model.
- o **Batch Normalization**: This technique helps stabilize the learning process by normalizing the activations in the network, speeding up convergence.
- o **Dropout Layers**: Dropout is applied to prevent overfitting by randomly disabling a fraction of neurons during training.
- o **Dense Layers**: Fully connected layers are used at the end of the network to perform classification based on the extracted features.
- o **Activation Functions**: The **ReLU** activation function is applied after each convolutional layer to introduce non-

linearity, and a **softmax** function is used in the final layer to output the probability distribution over the seven expression classes.

### 3.4.2 Transfer Learning

To improve the performance of the model, **transfer learning** was employed using a pre-trained model. By using weights from a model pre-trained on the **ImageNet** dataset, the CNN can learn to detect complex features without needing an enormous amount of training data. Fine-tuning this model on the FER dataset further enhanced its classification accuracy.

### 3.4.3 Hyperparameters and Optimizations

- **Optimizer**: The **RMSprop** optimizer was chosen for training, as it adapts the learning rate for each parameter and works well with the stochastic nature of deep learning.
- **Loss Function**: **Categorical cross-entropy** was used as the loss function since this is a multi-class classification problem.
- **Callbacks**: Early stopping and learning rate reduction were implemented to prevent overfitting and optimize the learning process.

### 3.5 Results and Discussion

### 3.5.1 Evaluation Metrics

The performance of the proposed model was evaluated using the following metrics:
- **Accuracy**: The proportion of correctly classified samples among the total samples.
- **Precision**: The ratio of true positives to the sum of true positives and false positives, reflecting the model's ability to avoid false positives.
- **Recall**: The ratio of true positives to the sum of true positives and false  negatives, indicating how well the model identifies positive instances.
- **F1-Score**: The harmonic mean of precision and recall, providing a balanced measure of both.

- **Confusion Matrix**: This matrix visually represents the distribution of predictions across different classes, helping to understand where the model struggles.

### 3.5.2 Experimental Results

The model was tested on a validation dataset with images labeled as one of the seven expressions: **angry, disgust, fear, happy, neutral, sad**, and **surprise**. The results of the performance evaluation, including **accuracy, precision, recall**, and **F1-score**, are summarized in **Table 3.1**, which provides a comprehensive view of all the metrics for each expression. Additionally, **Figures 3.1** through **3.4** offer a detailed analysis of each expression's performance in terms of **accuracy, precision, recall**, and **F1-score**, respectively, allowing for a clearer understanding of the model's performance across different metrics.

### Table 3.1

| Expression | Accuracy (%) | Precision (%) | Recall (%) | F1-Score (%) |
|---|---|---|---|---|
| Angry | 85.3 | 82.5 | 84.7 | 83.6 |
| Disgust | 78.6 | 77.1 | 79.0 | 78.0 |
| Fear | 84.1 | 83.0 | 82.9 | 82.9 |
| Happy | 90.2 | 92.5 | 91.3 | 91.9 |
| Neutral | 88.5 | 86.8 | 89.0 | 87.9 |
| Sad | 84.6 | 83.3 | 85.0 | 84.1 |
| Surprise | 91.7 | 93.2 | 92.0 | 92.6 |

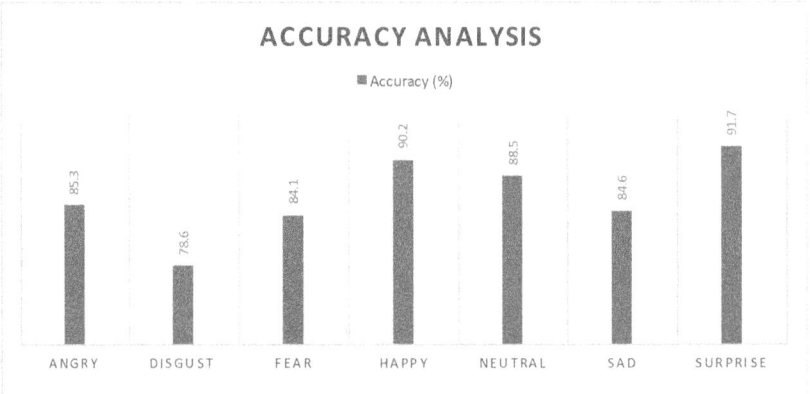

**Figure 3.1**

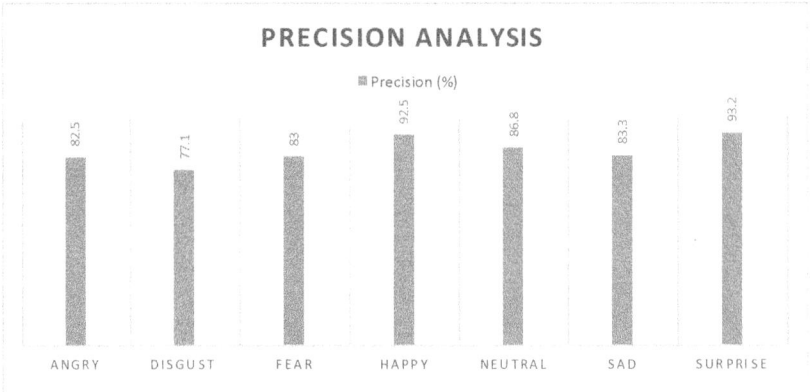

**Figure 3.2**

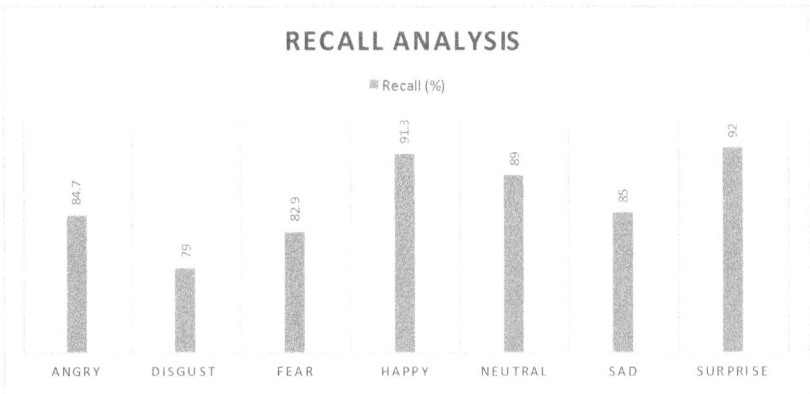

**Figure 3.3**

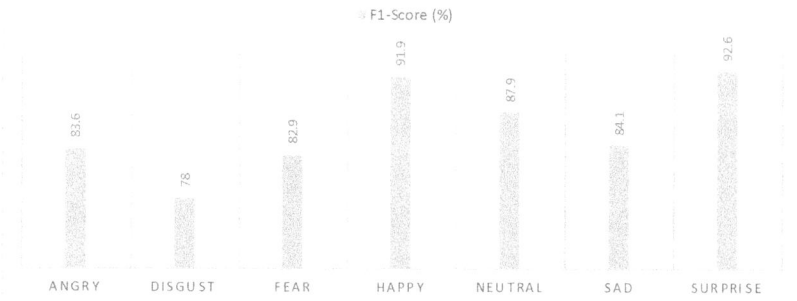

## F1-SCORE ANALYSIS

F1-Score (%)

| | | | | | | |
|---|---|---|---|---|---|---|
| 83.6 | 78 | 82.9 | 91.9 | 87.9 | 84.1 | 92.6 |
| ANGRY | DISGUST | FEAR | HAPPY | NEUTRAL | SAD | SURPRISE |

**Figure 3.4**

### 3.5.3 Discussion

- **Happy** and **surprise** expressions achieved the highest precision and recall values, with both metrics above 90%, which indicates that the model effectively recognizes these expressions with minimal false positives and negatives. This can be attributed to the distinctiveness of these emotions, making them easier for the model to classify.
- **Sad** and **angry** expressions showed relatively lower accuracy, precision, and recall, likely due to the more subtle visual differences between these expressions. This suggests the need for further training with more diverse datasets or enhanced preprocessing techniques to better differentiate these emotions.
- **Disgust** had the lowest performance in terms of precision and recall. This could be due to a smaller representation in the dataset or ambiguity between disgust and other negative emotions like fear or anger.
- The overall **F1-scores** indicate a balanced performance across all expressions, with the model achieving an average F1-score above 83%. This demonstrates that the proposed CNN model is effective at recognizing facial expressions but can benefit from further refinement, particularly in distinguishing more similar emotions like **sad** and **angry**.

## Conclusion

In this work, we have presented a CNN-based approach for facial expression recognition using the FER dataset. By integrating data augmentation and transfer learning, the model was able to achieve significant accuracy in classifying expressions. This approach demonstrates the potential for real-time facial expression recognition in various applications, from mental health diagnostics to emotion-driven user interfaces.

Future work will focus on optimizing the model for edge devices, enabling real-time processing in embedded systems. Additionally, expanding the dataset to include more diverse faces and expressions could further improve the generalization of the model.

## References

1. Xing Zhang, Lijun Yin, JeffreyF. Cohn, Shaun Canavan, Michael Reale, Andy Horowitz, Peng Liu, Jeffrey M. Girard (2014). BP4D-Spontaneous: A high-resolution spontaneous 3D dynamic facial expression database. *Image and Vision Computing*, 32(10), 692-706.
2. Ian Goodfellow, Yoshua Bengio, and Aaron Courville (2016). *Deep learning* (Vol. 1). Cambridge: MIT press.
3. Kaiming He, Xiangyu Zhang, Shaoqing Ren, Jian Sun (2016). Deep residual learning for image recognition. In *Proceedings of the IEEE conference on computer vision and pattern recognition* (pp. 770-778).
4. Paul Viola, Michael J. Jones (2001). Rapid object detection using a boosted cascade of simple features. Proceedings of the IEEE Conference on Computer Vision and Pattern Recognition (CVPR), 1, 511-518.
5. Paul Ekman, Wallace V. Friesen (1978). Facial action coding system: A technique for the measurement of facial movement. Consulting Psychologists Press.
6. Ali Mollahosseini, Behzad Hasani, Mohammad H. Mahoor (2016). AffectNet: A database for facial expression, valence, and arousal computing in the wild. IEEE Transactions on Affective Computing.

7. Gil Levi, Tal Hassner (2015). Emotion recognition in the wild via convolutional neural networks and mapped binary patterns. Proceedings of the ACM International Conference on Multimodal Interaction (pp. 503- 510).

8. Shan Li, Weihong Deng (2020). Deep facial expression recognition: A survey. IEEE Transactions on Affective Computing.

9. Zhou Yu, Cha Zhang (2015). Image-based static facial expression recognition with multiple deep network learning. Proceedings of the ACM International Conference on Multimodal Interaction (pp. 435-442).

10. Yi Fan, Xiaodong Lu, Dapeng Li, Yong Liu (2016). Video-based emotion recognition using CNN-RNN and C3D hybrid networks. Proceedings of the International Conference on Multimodal Interaction (pp. 445-452).

11. Özge Küntay, Hakan Can, Serkan Apaydın (2021). Comparative analysis of deep learning models for facial emotion recognition. IEEE Access, 9, 117084-117097.

12. Yichuan Tang (2013). Deep learning using linear support vector machines. arXiv preprint arXiv:1306.0239.

13. Kaipeng Zhang, Zhanpeng Zhang, Zhifeng Li, Yu Qiao (2016). Joint face detection and alignment using multitask cascaded convolutional networks. IEEE Signal Processing Letters, 23(10), 1499-1503.

14. Alex Krizhevsky, Ilya Sutskever, Geoffrey E. Hinton (2012). ImageNet classification with deep convolutional neural networks. Advances in Neural Information Processing Systems (pp. 1097-1105).

15. Min Liu, Ruifeng Wang (2017). Facial expression recognition based on fusion features of deep CNN. Journal of Electrical Engineering and Automation, 3(2), 36-42.

# Chapter 4

## Mask Detection and Social Distance Tracking using LBPH and Haar Cascade Algorithms

Sheelavathi A[1], P. Shanmugapriya[2], V. Mohan[3] and Muthukarupaee K[4]

[1,4]Department of Information Technology, Saranathan College of Engineering, Tiruchirappalli, India
[2,3]Department of ECE, Saranathan College of Engineering, Tiruchirappalli, India

### Abstract

### Face Mask Detection

Checking for face masks on customers' faces in a shop is known as face mask detection. Upon entering the store, the individual will be scanned by the system to determine if they are wearing a mask or not. A warning will be sent out to the person to wear a mask if they choose not to. Prior to identifying the features of their face, such as their lips and nose, the system will first detect their face. The system determines that the consumer is wearing a mask if it detects movement in the mouth, nose, and face. It will trigger an alert stating that they should wear a mask if it detects a face but not the mouth or nose.

### Tracking the social distancing

The focal length and sensor measurements of the intended camera must be entered by the user. The next step requires the user to place these two people at the minimum social distance that must be maintained; this distance is now known as the reference social distance. This has the benefit that authorities can choose the exact social distance they want to be maintained based on the rules they want to adhere to. For instance, according to WHO criteria, social distance should be at least 3 feet, but according to CDC guidelines, it should be at least 6 feet. It is not necessary to give the model the absolute distance when judging the social distance between two individuals. It is just evaluated in relation to the original calibration.

This social distancing concept is based on the idea that an image is essentially captured on the screen and that a camera lens is essentially a convex lens. As previously stated, the focal length and sensor measurements are required for this model. The distance between a lens's optic centers to its focus is known as its focal length. The focus length in optics and photography is expressed in millimeters (mm).

**Keywords:** Machine learning (ML), Local Binary Pattern Histogram(LBPH), Open Computer Vision(Open CV), You Only Look Once(YOLO), Face Mask, Mask Detection, Social Distance.

## 4.1 Introduction

This particular strain of pneumonia first appeared in the early months of December 2019 in the vicinity of Wuhan City, Hubei Province, China. On March 11, 2020, the World Health Organization (WHO) proclaimed it to be a global pandemic [1].Among many other symptoms, fever, dry cough, and exhaustion are the most typical corona virus symptoms. It primarily spreads by close, direct contact between individuals who have respiratory droplets from an infected person exhaled, sneezed, or coughed. Because these droplets fall swiftly on floors or other surfaces and are too dense to swing in the air for extended periods of time, the virus can also spread when people touch infected surfaces and then touch their own face, including the eyes, nose, and mouth [2].

The World Health Organization (WHO) has imposed a state of emergency worldwide and has devised emergency precautionary measures to curb the virus's spread. These include frequent hand washing with soap and water for twenty seconds, the use of hand sanitizers, maintaining a safe distance, routinely disinfecting surfaces, using disposable tissues for coughing and sneezing, and—above all—wearing face masks in public areas [3, 4].similar to successfully stopping the SARS virus from spreading throughout the community during the 2003 SARS outbreak [5]

It has also been demonstrated that using face masks for the entire community is very successful in preventing the transmission of the corona virus [6–10]. Since masks effectively limit respiratory droplets, mask wear has been a hallmark of the COVID-19 response. For example, N95 and surgical masks are 91% and 68% effective in preventing the spread of viruses, respectively, by obstructing respiratory droplets [11,12]. By using a face mask, one can successfully block the spread of airborne viruses and particles, preventing some pollutants from entering another person's respiratory system [13].

During the COVID-19 pandemic, we must take precautions to stop the disease from spreading. We primarily need to wear face masks. Individuals are gathering within the stores and are unable to keep their distance from one another. Our project's primary objective is to identify facial masks in moving photos or videos and notify shoppers if a group of individuals has assembled within a mall. In order to ensure that people are adhering to these safety procedures, we have created a facemask detecting system. After detecting the face, it will determine whether or not the wearer is wearing a mask. This technique will discern between the faces wearing masks and those that don't. A higher number of faces spotted at close range notify the system that social separation is not being observed.

## 4.2 Features of Mask Detection System and Social Distance Maintenance

The main issue with this epidemic is keeping track of who is wearing masks and who isn't. This system will recognize faces and determine whether or not they are wearing masks. Consequently, this technique will aid in stopping the fatal sickness from spreading among people. When multiple faces are identified at close ranges during face detection, the system is notified that social distancing is not being upheld.

When a face is detected, age and gender are determined. This aids in limiting both the overall and inside-the-mall count of elderly individuals. This allows them to freely make purchases without being surrounded by people inside the store or mall. Assuring that masks are checked, and samples of people's images are saved when they are within the mall, helps to create reports that can be retrieved whenever needed.

## Existing System

The existing method uses CNN (Convolutional Neural Network) in Deep Learning for face mask detection and recognition. In public places with high traffic density, such as train stations, airports, etc., facial recognition and detection are used to identify offenders. Owing to the pandemic, it is imperative to check face masks, and this is done by labor. In a store or mall, paid labor is utilized to verify whether customers are wearing masks, although doing so puts workers at risk of infection.

Drawbacks are:

1. Takes up more space
2. High labor costs

**Proposed System**

This method aids in keeping people apart and preventing the COVID virus from spreading. When a specific person enters the mall, their face is first recognized using a mask, and then their age and gender are determined. The shopping mall's entry and exit systems are connected to this system. Once a customer's face is identified, a database with all of their faces is generated. A system at the entrance area counts each individual who enters, and the mall can only accommodate 50 people at a time. It will inform them when they go above the limit. IoT will be used to carry out this alert message's following actions (if indicated).

Following the alarm message, individuals are prohibited from entering until the count is reduced. The face of the individual exiting will be recognized by the system. The count on the entry camera will go down if the face matches the face in the database. After that, it prompts someone else to enter the mall.

**Advantages**

1. It takes a lot of time to complete. For developers, this frees up a lot of time to be used in more productive ways.
2. Technical supporter is sufficient to keep the system up to date.
3. Compared to labor costs, maintenance costs are lower.

**4.3 Related Works**

The authors of [14] provided for Identifying and monitoring terrorists or criminals is made possible by the ability to accurately and efficiently recognize masked faces. Because of significant occlusions that cause the loss of facial characteristics, masked face identification is a unique face detection problem that is quite challenging.

This makes masked face detection much more challenging because there are very few large-scale, well annotated masked face datasets available. Deep learning algorithms based on CNN have achieved significant advancements in various domains of computer vision, such as facial recognition. In order to detect masked faces, they provide a novel CNN-based cascade framework in this paper. It comprises of three convolutional neural networks that have been meticulously developed. Additionally, in order to improve our CNN models, they suggest a new dataset named the "MASKED FACE dataset" due to the dearth of masked face training examples. Our suggested masked face detection technique performs satisfactorily when tested on the MASKED FACE testing set. The limitation of this method is that it can only be operated successfully after utilizing a fine-tuned model in the dataset.

The goal of the project is to use a security camera to automatically reveal a masked person in real time [15]. The primary goal is to use the Viola Jones Algorithm to automatically identify masked individuals in a shorter amount of time.

In this work, the researcher presents a four-step variant method that includes estimating the person's distance from the camera, detecting the eye line, detecting facial parts like the mouth, and finally detecting the face. If the person's eyes are identified during face detection and then their face is identified, it means that their face is not covered by a mask. Because of this novel approach to the issue, a transparent and simpler technique of solving it has been developed, making real-time implementation more advantageous and feasible. The drawbacks of this method are that it is light-sensitive and may give an incorrect result if the face is more light-colored.

For our project [16], we've used the Haar Cascade and Local Binary Pattern histogram to recognize faces. For face recognition in this project, the Haar Cascade and Local Binary Pattern Histogram were utilized. The suggested Attendance system uses LBPH for facial recognition and haar cascade for face detection. Features offered by this technology include the ability to take pictures of students and train those photographs in a database. We have 60 examples of individual student photos in our dataset. In the face identification process, the color frame is converted to grayscale in order to identify the faces.

To train and detect features in images, such as lines and eyes, the Haar Cascade feature is employed. We select the Local Binary Pattern for Face Recognition, which produces a picture that more effectively highlights the image's features. Compared to eigenfaces and Fisher faces, it is more adept at identifying both side and front faces. Compared to other algorithms, it performs better in a variety of settings and lighting circumstances. As soon as the system recognizes an image, it shows the image's ID from the dataset that was saved during face identification matching the identified image.

In recent times [17], facial recognition technology has gained substantial popularity. It's too difficult because of face changes and the existence of multiple masks. Masking is another prevalent occurrence in the real world when someone is not cooperative with the technology, like in video surveillance.

The present face recognition performance suffers for these masks. Numerous studies have been conducted to identify faces in a variety of settings, such as difficult lighting or stance, deteriorated photos, etc. Nonetheless, mask-related issues are typically ignored. The main goal of this effort is to improve the accuracy of recognizing various masked faces, with a focus on facial masks. A workable method that starts with face region detection has been suggested.

## 4.4 Incorporated Packages

### TensorFlow

TensorFlow is an interface used to express machine learning algorithms that is used to implement machine learning systems into fabrication across many computer science domains, such as computer vision, sentiment analysis, voice recognition, geographic information extraction, text summarization, information retrieval, computational drug discovery, and flaw detection for research purposes [18].

TensorFlow is used as the backend of the Sequential CNN architecture in the suggested model, which consists of many layers. It is also employed in data processing to restructure the data -image.

**Keras**

Keras provides basic reflections and building blocks for the rapid design and delivery of machine learning setups. It makes complete use of TensorFlow's cross-platform and scalability features. Models and layers make up Keras' fundamental data structures [19]. Keras is utilized in the implementation of every layer in the CNN model. It assists in assembling the entire model in addition to converting the class vector to the binary class matrix in data processing.

**OpenCV**

An open-source computer vision and machine learning software library called OpenCV (Open Source Computer Vision Library) is used to distinguish and identify faces, identify objects, group movements in recordings, trace progressive modules, follow eye gestures, track camera actions, remove red eyes from flash-taken photos, find similar images from an image database, perceive landscapes and place markers to overlay them with more realism, and other tasks [20]. The suggested technique uses these OpenCV features to convert the color and resize data images.

**4.5 System Design**

Making computers think like humans is a process known as machine learning. The computer program that uses historical data to optimize performance is called machine learning. The computer must be trained in order for it to think like a person. Numerous algorithms are available for training. In this case, we use the LBPH and Haarcascade algorithms. Another name for the Haarcascade technique is the Viola-Jones technique. This algorithm aids in both face detection and recognition as well as face mask inspection. The fundamental issue in this epidemic is determining whether or not people use masks and maintain social distance. In fact, shops are the only places where we can see a larger crowd. So, we're trying to determine whether or not the people who enter the stores are wearing masks, and we're also going to look at their social distance.

We use the Haarcascade and LBPH algorithms for face detection and recognition. LBPH stands for Local Binary Pattern Histogram. The Haarcascade method uses haar characteristics to detect faces. It will look for traits such as eyes, nose, and mouth to establish its identity as a face. After detecting the face, we will inspect the mask on the face. To check whether a person is wearing a mask, we use an XML file. The equipment will inspect the nose and mouth. If it detects both features, it will notify them to wear masks via an alert message. If not, it will deduce that the person wears a mask.

The system architecture outlines how the planned system will function, as shown in Figure 2. We first detect the face using a webcam and then look for masks in the face. Furthermore, we perform face recognition utilizing the photos recorded in the dataset during face detection.

**Face detection**

We used the Haarcascade technique to detect the faces. First, the web camera will detect faces, and then 50 sample photographs will be put in the dataset. We can crop the detected face as necessary. This face will be further trained by the system.First, we convert the frame from color to grayscale. To detect faces, we utilized a Haar Cascade classifier, which trains a cascade function and detects features in subsequent images. For this, we use Haar characteristics such as edge, line, and four rectangles. A huge or variable-sized image requires a lot of calculation and attributes, the majority of which are unimportant. The Region of Interest (ROI), which contains faces, is extracted and moved to the next stage.

Face recognition is used here at the shop's exit. The face will be recognized by the exit side webcam using the LBPH (Local Binary Pattern Histogram) algorithm. It will determine whether the face identified by the departure camera is included in the collection, in which we have previously archived sample photos of the faces identified by the entering camera.

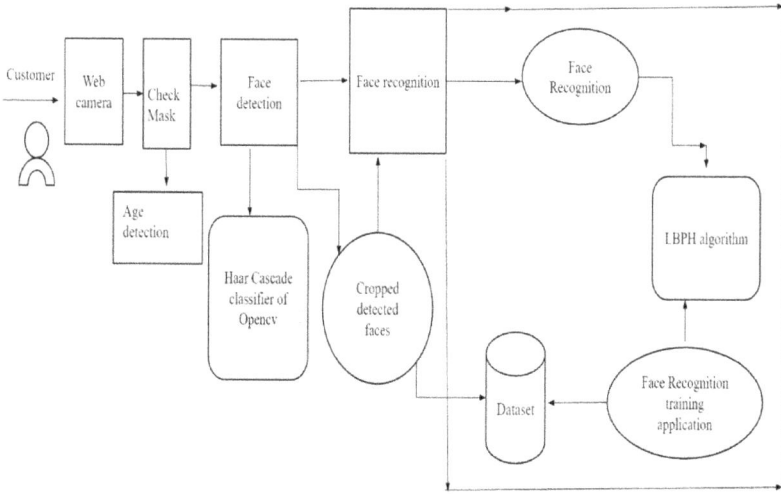

**Figure 4.1** System architecture.

We chose the LBPH algorithm for face recognition due to its resilience, ability to identify side and front faces, and superiority over Eigenfaces and Fisherfaces. In order to identify the features that most accurately depict a face in an image, the LBPH algorithm is employed. The LBPH method outperforms the other face recognition algorithms. This approach is simpler because it characterizes the image in the dataset locally [18]. When an unknown image replaces an existing image, we run an analogous algorithm and compare the output to every image in the dataset. Compared to other algorithms, it performs better in a variety of settings and lighting circumstances.

The Local Binary Pattern (LBP) operation produces an image that more effectively showcases an image's features. It makes use of the radius, neighbors, and sliding window concepts. The frame is first transformed into 3x3 pixel matrices. assign the value to 1 in a matrix if a neighboring pixel is larger than the matrix's median pixel. otherwise, assign the value to 0 at that pixel position. Next, record the values of adjacent pixels in a line so that we can obtain a binary number. Replace the binary integer with the matrix's median pixel value after converting it to decimal[20].Now that the image is in LBP form, we take the histograms out of each grid and combine them to create a new, bigger histogram. The original image's attributes are displayed by the concatenated histogram. The facial image

51

is represented by each histogram. Every histogram depicts a face image taken from the database. It follows the above procedures for the new image and obtains a new histogram for it.

## Mask Check

Here, we will ascertain whether or not the individual entering the store is wearing a mask. We will use the Haarcascade XML file to identify a person's mouth and nose as part of the validation process. If the nose and mouth are detected by the system, it indicates that the person is not wearing a mask. Thus, a warning to wear a mask will be displayed. The wearer is wearing a mask if the system cannot identify their mouth or nose. The person donned a mask, according to the system currently. The mask check is shown in Figure 4.2. We must divide our project into two independent stages, each with individual sub-steps, in order to train a custom face mask detector:

1. Training: The main goals of this step are to load the face mask detection dataset from disk, train a model on it using Tensor Flow, and serialize the face mask detector to disk.
2. Deployment: Following face detection and training, we can load the mask detector, classify each face as having a mask on or not, and perform face detection.

In order to identify the person in the picture, the new histogram is now compared to the histograms from the training dataset using Euclidian distance. The histogram with the lowest confidence, or the least distance, is selected because lower confidence is preferable, and the ID associated with that histogram is also extracted. Details pertaining to the retrieved ID are on the frame if the confidence level is less than fifty. To prevent duplicate names, the names are updated in the excel spreadsheet. This aids in identifying the shop's intruders.

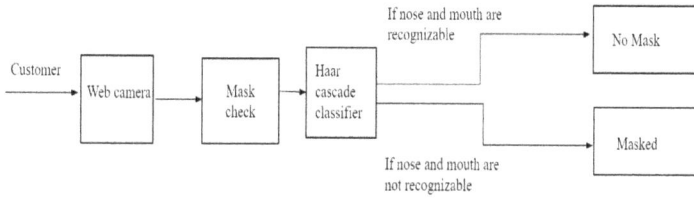

**Figure 4.2** Mask check.

**How was our face mask dataset created?**

1. Taking standard portraits of faces
2. After that, unique Python computer software is made to add face masks.

The location of face structures, such as the eyes and eyebrows, can be automatically inferred through facial landmarks. In order to create a dataset of people wearing face masks using facial landmarks, we must first begin with a picture of a person who is not wearing a face mask. After that, we use face detection to determine where the image's face's bounding box is. The face Region of Interest can be extracted once we determine the location of the face inside the image. The eyes, nose, mouth, and other features can then be localized by applying face landmarks.

**Tracking Social Distancing**
The user must enter the focal length and sensor measurements of the intended camera. The next step is for the user to place these two people at the minimal social distance that needs to be maintained. this is known as the reference social distance. The benefit of this is that authorities can choose the exact norms they intend to adhere to, as well as the social distance they want maintained. For instance, according to CDC and WHO rules, the minimum social distance should be six feet, although three feet is the suggested minimum. The idea behind this social distance model is that an image is essentially captured on the screen, and a camera lens is just a convex lens. As previously stated, the focal length and sensor measurements are required for this model [21]. The distance between a lens's optic center to its focus is known as its focal length. The focus

length in optics and photography is expressed in millimeters (mm). Higher magnification is achieved with a longer focal length, but the angle of view is reduced.

A component of a camera's hardware called an image sensor uses light to detect information and turn a view into an image. In essence, the sensor is a screen onto which every pixel in a picture is transferred. Higher the quality of the image, the more mapped pixels there are. Let field width, or the measured distance an object is from the camera be d, and the observed width of an object in real life be w. Let Persons 1 and 2 be the persons between whom the distance is being measured. They should be located at coordinates (x1, y1) and (x2, y2) in the accompanying image. These locations can be found at the people's feet.

Sensor_dimension / focal_length = field_dimension / distance_field ---(1)

Equation 2 can be utilized to get the following formula for determining an object's depth in a photograph:

d = real obj_height (mm) x focal_length (mm) / obj_height on sensor (mm) ---(2)

Where obj is an object. The following formula can be used to determine the height of the object in the image on the sensor in millimeters, as we only know the object's height in pixels (px) in the image. Since the average height of a human is thought to be that match, the height of a real human is supposed to be 1.6 meters in this model.

obj-height on sensor(mm) =obj_height in image(Px.)x pixel size ---(3)

Where Px is the measurement in pixel count. Therefore, the depth of an individual would be equivalent to their distance from the camera. The two people's distances from the camera will be shown as d1 and d2. The difference in these two individuals' x-coordinates is considered to be the social distance width, which is used to calculate the proper distance between them in the picture.

$$\text{width(mm) of social distancing} = (|x1 - x2|) \times \text{pixel size} \qquad \text{---(4)}$$

$$w = \text{sensor\_width} \times \text{width of social distancing} / \text{focal\_len(mm)} \qquad \text{---(5)}$$

Assuming that person 1 is at (0, d1) and person 2 is at (w, d2)

$$\text{Social distancing} = [(w - 0)^2 + (d2 - d1)^2]^2 \qquad \text{---(6)}$$

The following formula (7) has to be applied in order to determine the pixel size:

$$\text{Pixel\_ size} = \text{sensor\_width(mm)/img\_width (px)} + \text{sensor\_height(mm)/img\_height (px)} /2 \text{ ---(7)}$$

The reference social distance will be the social distance that is initially computed in calibration mode. In testing mode, the equations will be used to determine the social distance between two people. The two people will be marked as violators if the computed social distance is smaller than the reference social distance.

## YOLOV3

The most recent version of the well-known object detection system YOLO, or "You Only Look Once," is called YOLOV3. Most notably, the released model is extremely quick and almost as accurate as single shot Multibox(SSD) while still being able to identify 80 distinct items in pictures and videos[19]. The image is first divided into a 13 by 13 grid of cells.

Depending on the size of the input, these 169 cells have different sizes. 32 x 32 boxes made up each cell in the image for the 416 by 416 input size that we used in our research. The likelihood that an object enclosed by a bounding box belongs to a specific class and the bounding box's confidence are also predicted by the network for each bounding box. The majority of these bounding boxes are removed either because they enclose the same object as another bounding box with a very high confidence score, or because their confidence is low. Non-maximum suppression is the term for this method.

## Conclusion

One of the viruses that is spreading quickly and endangering people's health as well as international trade and the economy is COVID-19. Controlling the issue was challenging due to the rapid pace of mutation and dissemination. Wearing a face mask in public spaces is one of the most crucial preventive steps that can help stop the virus from spreading. We suggested utilizing machine learning to detect social separation and facial masks. The goal of the project was to make sure it could hold up in the difficult actual world of today. Its potential is enormous.

## References

[1] Fong S. J., Dey N., and Chaki J., An introduction to covid-19, In Artificial intelligence for coronavirus outbreak, 2021, Springer, Singapore, 1–22.

[2] Vaishya R., Javaid M., Khan I. H., and Haleem A., Artificial intelligence (ai) applications for covid-19 pandemic, Diabetes & Metabolic Syndrome: Clinical Research & Reviews. (2020) 14, no. 4, 337–339, https://doi.org/10.1016/j.dsx.2020.04.012, 32305024.

[3] Bhagat S., Yadav N., Shah J., Dave H., Swaraj S., Tripathi S., and Singh S., Novel corona virus (covid-19) pandemic: current status and possible strategies for detection and treatment of the disease, Expert Review of Anti-Infective Therapy, 2020, Taylor & Francis, 1–24, https://doi.org/10.1080/14787210.2021.1835469.

[4] Xiao Y. and Torok M. E., Taking the right measures to control covid-19, The Lancet Infectious Diseases. (2020) 20, no. 5, 523–524, https://doi.org/10.1016/S1473-3099(20)30152-3, 32145766.

[5] Peng P. W. H., Wong D. T., Bevan D., and Gardam M., Infection control and anesthesia: lessons learned from the toronto sars outbreak, Canadian Journal of Anesthesia. (2003) 50, no. 10, 989–997, https://doi.org/10.1007/BF03018361, 2-s2.0-0942266301, 14656775.

[6] Cheng V. C.-C., Wong S.-C., Chuang V. W.-M., So S. Y.-C., Chen J. H.-K., Sridhar S., To K. K.-W., Chan J. F.-W., Hung I. F.-N., Ho P. L., and Yuen K.-Y., The role of community-wide wearing of face mask for control of coronavirus disease 2019 (covid-19) epidemic due to

sars-cov-2, Journal of Infection. (2020) 81, no. 1, 107 114, https://doi.org/10.1016/j.jinf.2020.04.024, 32335167.

[7] Steffen E., Eikenberry M. M., Iboi E., Phan T., Eikenberry K., Kuang Y., Kostelich E., and Gumel A. B., To mask or not to mask: modeling the potential for face mask use by the general public to curtail the covid-19 pandemic, Infectious Disease Modelling. (2020) 5, 293–308.

[8] Cook T. M., Personal protective equipment during the coronavirus disease (covid) 2019 pandemic–a narrative review, Anaesthesia. (2020) 75, no. 7, 920–927, https://doi.org/10.1111/anae.15071.

[9] Greenhalgh T., Schmid M. B., Czypionka T., Bassler D., and Gruer L., Face masks for the public during the covid-19 crisis, BMJ. (2020) 369, https://doi.org/10.1136/bmj.m1435.

[10] Matuschek C., Moll F., Fangerau H., Fischer J. C., Zänker K., van Griensven M., Schneider M., KindgenMilles D., Knoefel W. T., Lichtenberg A., and Tamaskovics B., Face masks: benefits and risks during the covid-19 crisis, European Journal of Medical Research. (2020) 25, no. 1, 1–8.

[11] Li T., Liu Y., Li M., Qian X., and Dai S. Y., Mask or no mask for covid-19: a public health and market study, PloS one. (2020) 15, no. 8, article e0237691, https://doi.org/10.1371/journal.pone.0237691, 327970 67.

[12] Longrich N. R. and Sheppard S. K., Publicuse of masks to control the coronavirus pandemic, 2020, preprints.org.

[13] Qin B. and Li D., Identifying facemask-wearing condition using image super-resolution with classification network to prevent covid-19, Sensors. (2020) 20, no. 18, https://doi.org/10.3390/s20185236, 32937867.

[14] Wei Bu, Jiangjian Xiao, Chuanhong Zhou, Minmin Yang, ChengbinPeng "A Cascade Framework for Masked Face Detection" 2017.

[15] Aishwarya Radhakrishnan Nair, Dr. Amol D. Potgantwar Savitabai Phule "Masked Face Detection using the Viola Jones Algorithm" 2017.

[16] Bharath Tej Chinimilli, Anjali T, Akhil Kotturi, Vihas Reddy Kaipu, Jathin Varma Mandapati, "Face Recognition based Attendance System using Haar Cascade and Local Binary Pattern Histogram", 2020

[17] Md. Sabbir Ejaz and Md. Rabiul Islam "Masked face recognition using convolutional neural network" 2019.

[18] G B Huang, H Lee, E L. Miller, "Learning hierarchical representation for Face verification with convolution deep belief networks[C]", Proceedings of International Conference on Computer Vision and Pattern Recognition,pp.223-226,2012.

[19] Computer Vision Papers, http://www.cvpapers.com

[20] P. Dollar, V. Rabaud, G. Cottrell, and S. Belongie, "Behavior recognition ´ via sparse spatio-temporal features," in 2005 IEEE International Workshop on Visual Surveillance and Performance Evaluation of Tracking and Surveillance. IEEE, 2005, pp. 65–72.

[21] K.J. Wang, SH.L. Duan & W.X. Feng (2008), "A Survey of Face Recognition using Single Training Sample", Pattern Recognition and Artificial Intelligence, China, Vol. 21, Pp. 635–642.

# Chapter 5

## Computerized Cognitive Retraining Program for Home training of Children with Disabilities – A Learning App

**SenthamilSelvi R, Dineshkumar P, Alaagammai S, Cauvery R, Deepika S and Kiruthika K**[6]
Dept of CSE, Saranathan College of Engineering, Tamil Nadu, India

### Abstract

The aim of this chapter is to present an app for children with disabilities so that they can get a retraining program at home without any one to monitor them. Here we mainly focus on three deficiencies affecting the majority of children: dyslexia, dysgraphia and dyscalculia. We have included different levels of games namely primary, secondary, and tertiary, and each level has many types of games recommended by doctors such as Balloon Bob Game, Big Floor Puzzles, and Group story. We perform facial recognition by using algorithms. The app is completely automatic and guides the children using their favorite cartoon characters it generates overall performance report every month. The system moves to next game only when a score of at least 50% for each level is attained. To encourage physical activity, the app suggests performing the activity which is monitored using the camera and report is generated.

**Keywords:** Facial recognition, Assistive Technology, Progress Monitoring, Physical activity monitoring.

### 5.1 Introduction
The proposed project aims to develop an innovative app designed to support children with learning disabilities, specifically targeting conditions such as dyslexia, dysgraphia, and dyscalculia.

Dyslexia:
Dyslexia is a specific learning disorder that primarily affects an individual's ability to read, spell, write, and sometimes speak. It is not related to intelligence but involves difficulties in processing lan-

guage. People with dyslexia often have trouble recognizing and decoding words, which can lead to challenges with reading fluency and comprehension. However, they often excel in other areas, such as problem-solving, creativity, and thinking in nonlinear ways.

Dysgraphia:
Dysgraphia is a learning disability that primarily affects a person's ability to write coherently and legibly. It involves difficulties with handwriting, spelling, and organizing thoughts on paper. Dysgraphia does not affect a person's intelligence but rather their ability to translate thoughts into written words and symbols. This condition can be particularly challenging for school-aged children, as it interferes with many academic tasks requiring written output.

Dyscalculia:
Dyscalculia is a learning disorder that affects an individual's ability to understand and perform mathematical tasks. People with dyscalculia often struggle with number-related concepts, such as counting, recognizing numbers, understanding arithmetic operations, and grasping mathematical symbols. This condition is sometimes compared to dyslexia, but while dyslexia affects reading and language, dyscalculia specifically impacts math skills

The app provides an autonomous, home-based retraining program where children can engage in educational and developmental activities without the need for constant supervision. To cater to diverse needs, the app offers a series of games at varying difficulty levels—primary, secondary, and tertiary—that have been carefully curated and recommended by medical professionals.

In addition to gamified learning, the app integrates advanced facial recognition algorithms to track the child's engagement and emotional state, ensuring a personalized and responsive experience. With guidance from their favorite cartoon characters, children remain motivated while learning. Monthly performance reports are automatically generated and shared with both doctors and guardians, allowing for real-time adjustments based on feedback.

Furthermore, to encourage a holistic approach to development, the app suggests and monitors physical activities, ensuring that children are not only developing cognitively but also maintaining physical health. With its user-friendly, adaptive, and interactive design, this app aims to revolutionize how children with disabilities receive education and therapy, promoting independence and continuous growth in a fun, engaging environment.

## 5.2 Related Work

An app designed for children with learning disabilities, specifically targeting dyslexia, dysgraphia, and dyscalculia. The goal is to provide a retraining program that children can follow at home independently, without constant supervision. Key features of the app include:

Target Disabilities: The app focuses on children affected by dyslexia (difficulty with reading), dysgraphia (difficulty with writing), and dyscalculia (difficulty with math).

Game Based Learning: The app offers a series of educational games that cater to these disabilities, categorized into three levels: primary, secondary, and tertiary. These games are recommended by doctors and aim to improve cognitive and learning skills.

Examples of games include:
Balloon Bob Game: Likely a game that improves hand-eye coordination or focus.
Big Floor Puzzles: Puzzles to enhance problem-solving skills.
Group Story: A collaborative or imaginative storytelling game to improve literacy and communication.

Facial Recognition: Facial recognition algorithms are used to track and monitor the child's engagement, progress, or emotional state while using the app. This allows for a personalized experience and helps in adjusting difficulty levels or pacing.

Cartoon-Based Guidance: The app is designed to be child-friendly, using familiar and favorite cartoon characters to guide children through activities and keep them engaged.

Performance Monitoring: The app generates monthly performance reports based on the child's progress in the games. These reports are automatically shared with both doctors and guardians. Based on feedback from doctors or guardians, the app is adaptable to better suit the needs of the child.

Progression Rules: Children can only advance to the next level of games if they score at least 50% on the current level, ensuring they master basic skills before moving forward.

Encouragement of Physical Activity: In addition to cognitive exercises, the app promotes physical activities. The camera monitors these activities, and reports on the child's physical engagement are generated. This feature ensures the holistic development of the child, integrating physical movement alongside mental exercises.

## 5.3 Proposed System

The flowchart illustrates a proposed system designed to assist in the identification and management of learning disabilities, specifically dyslexia, dysgraphia, and dyscalculia. The system begins with a registration and login process, allowing users to access the platform. Once logged in, students are assessed for each of the three learning disabilities, with their levels categorized as basic, moderate, or advanced. This categorization is crucial for tailoring educational interventions to individual needs.

Following the assessments, the system generates comprehensive reports that summarize the student's strengths and weaknesses. These reports can be invaluable for educators, parents, and other stakeholders in developing effective strategies to support the student's learning. By providing a structured approach to identifying and addressing learning disabilities, this system aims to improve educational outcomes for students who may face challenges in traditional learning environments.

## 5.3.1 Proposed System Architecture

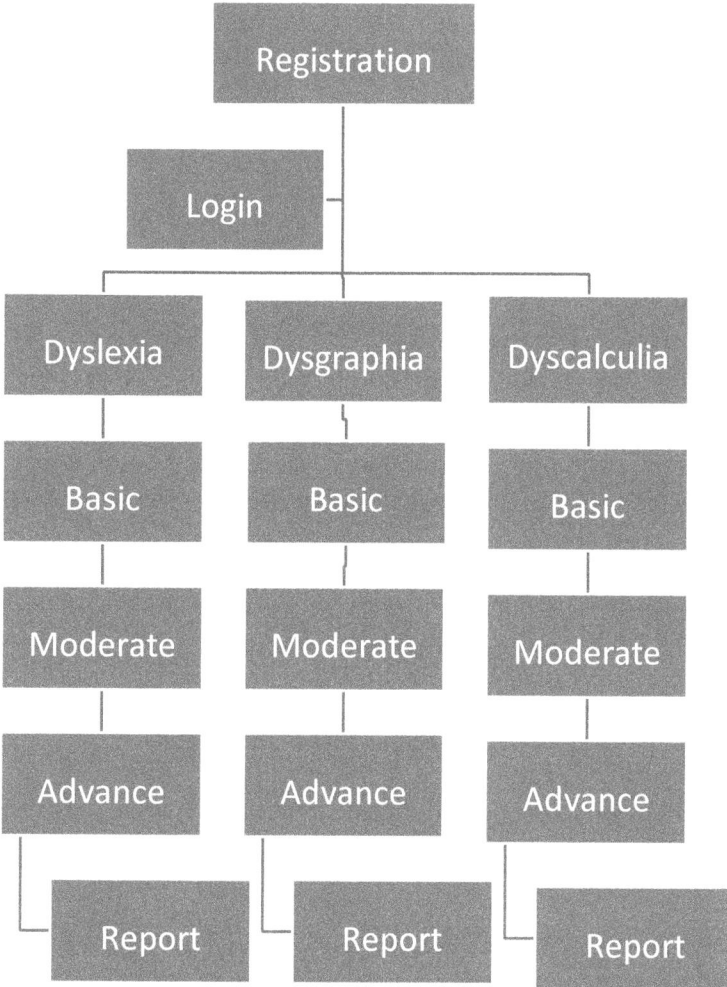

**Figure 5.1** Diagram of proposed method

## 5.3.2 Proposed System Working

### *Registration and Login*

The registration and login process in the proposed system serves as the gateway to accessing the platform for assessment and support.

This process ensures that only authorized users can utilize the system's features.

Registration:

New User Creation: Individuals who have not previously used the system can create a new account by providing necessary information. This typically includes:
* Full name
* Email address
* Password
* Contact information (e.g., phone number)
* Disease type (like Dyslexia, Dysgraphia, and Dyscalculia)

Account Verification: Upon successful registration, the system may send a verification email or code to the provided email address to confirm the account. This helps prevent unauthorized access.
Login:

Account Access: Existing users can log in to the system using their registered email address and password.

Authentication: The system verifies the provided credentials to ensure that the user is authorized to access the platform.

Session Management: Once a user successfully logs in, a session is established, allowing them to navigate and use the system's features until they log out.

The registration and login process is a standard security measure designed to protect user data and ensure that only authorized individuals can access the system's resources.

Example: A parent or Guardian creates a new account to access the system for his/her children to give a training for their disabilities

### Dyslexia, Dysgraphia, and Dyscalculia Assessments

The proposed system includes assessments for dyslexia, dysgraphia, and dyscalculia. These assessments are designed to evaluate specific skills related to reading, writing, and mathematics, respectively.

Dyslexia Assessment:
* Reading Fluency: Measures a student's ability to read words accurately and quickly.
* Decoding Skills: Evaluates a student's ability to break down words into their individual sounds and blend them together.
* Comprehension: Assesses a student's understanding of written text.
* Phonological Awareness: Measures a student's ability to identify and manipulate individual sounds in words.

Dysgraphia Assessment:
* Handwriting: Evaluates a student's handwriting skills, including letter formation, spacing, and legibility.
* Motor Skills: Assesses a student's fine motor skills, such as hand-eye coordination and finger dexterity.
* Spelling: Measures a student's ability to spell words accurately.
* Written Expression: Evaluates a student's ability to express ideas clearly and coherently in writing.

Dyscalculia Assessment:
* Number Sense: Measures a student's understanding of numbers and their relationships.
* Basic Arithmetic: Evaluates a student's ability to perform basic arithmetic operations (addition, subtraction, multiplication, and division).
* Problem-Solving: Assesses a student's ability to solve mathematical problems.

### Levels (Basic, Moderate, and Advanced Levels)

The proposed system categorizes students into three levels based on their performance on the assessments: basic, moderate, and advanced. These levels reflect the severity of the learning disability and guide the appropriate interventions.

Basic Level:

* Characteristics: Students at the basic level exhibit significant difficulties in the areas assessed. Their performance is well below grade-level expectations.
* Examples: A student with dyslexia at the basic level may have difficulty decoding words, reading fluently, and comprehending text. A student with dysgraphia at the basic level may struggle with handwriting, spelling, and written expression. A student with dyscalculia at the basic level may have difficulty with basic arithmetic operations, number sense, and problem-solving.

Game Suggestions:

* Sound Touch: Focus on simple sounds and basic identification.
* Favorites: Keep choices limited and focus on familiar options.
* Story Times: Use short, simple stories with clear visuals.
* Finger Trace and Rainbow Write: Start with simple letter shapes and focus on tactile exploration.
* Word Practice: Use basic vocabulary and simple word structures.
* Guess Me: Use a limited number of words and provide visual clues.
* Name Matchers: Use simple pictures and familiar names.
* Puzzles: Start with simple puzzles with few pieces.
* Cubes: Use simple puzzles with few pieces.

Moderate Level:

* Characteristics: Students at the moderate level exhibit significant difficulties, but they are able to perform some tasks with support. Their performance is below grade-level expectations.
* Examples: A student with dyslexia at the moderate level may have difficulty with complex texts and may require accommodations such as assistive technology. A student with dysgraphia at the moderate level may have difficulty with more complex writing tasks and may need support with spelling and grammar. A student with dyscalculia at the moderate level may have difficulty with multi-step problems and may need additional practice with arithmetic operations.

Game Suggestions:
* Sound Touch: Introduce more complex sounds and encourage discrimination.
* Favorites: Offer a wider range of choices and discuss preferences.
* Story Times: Use longer, more complex stories with richer vocabulary.
* Finger Trace and Rainbow Write: Introduce more complex letter shapes and encourage fine motor skills.
* Word Practice: Use more complex vocabulary and word structures.
* Guess Me: Increase the number of words and reduce visual clues.
* Name Matchers: Use more complex pictures and unfamiliar names.
* Puzzles: Use more complex puzzles with more pieces.
* Cubes: Use more complex puzzles with more pieces.

Advanced Level:
* Characteristics: Students at the advanced level exhibit significant difficulties, but they are able to perform some tasks independently. Their performance may be at or near grade-level expectations with accommodations.
* Examples: A student with dyslexia at the advanced level may require accommodations such as extended time or assistive technology for certain tasks. A student with dysgraphia at the advanced level may have difficulty with complex writing tasks and may need support with organization and planning. A student with dyscalculia at the advanced level may have difficulty with complex mathematical concepts and may need additional practice with problem-solving strategies.

Game Suggestions:
* Sound Touch: Introduce a variety of sounds and encourage identification and discrimination.
* Favorites: Encourage students to explain their preferences and justify their choices.
* Story Times: Use complex stories with rich vocabulary and themes.
* Finger Trace and Rainbow Write: Focus on handwriting fluency and speed.

* Word Practice: Use advanced vocabulary and complex word structures.
* Guess Me: Use a large number of words and minimal visual clues.
* Name Matchers: Use complex pictures and unfamiliar names.
* Puzzles: Use challenging puzzles with many pieces.
* Cubes: Use challenging puzzles with many pieces.

### Report Generation

The proposed system generates comprehensive reports that summarize a student's assessment results and provide insights into their strengths and weaknesses. These reports can be invaluable for educators, parents, and other stakeholders in developing effective strategies to support the student's learning.

Key Components of the Report:
* Student Information: Basic details about the student, such as name, age, and grade level.
* Assessment Results: A summary of the student's performance on the dyslexia, dysgraphia, and dyscalculia assessments, including scores and rankings.
* Strengths and Weaknesses: Identification of the student's areas of strength and areas where they may need additional support.
* Level of Difficulty: Categorization of the student's level of difficulty (basic, moderate, or advanced) for each learning disability.
* Recommendations: Suggestions for educational interventions, accommodations, and strategies to address the student's specific needs.

Purpose of the Report:
* Inform Stakeholders: Provide educators, parents, and other stakeholders with a clear understanding of the student's learning profile.
* Guide Interventions: Offer recommendations for targeted interventions to address the student's specific needs.
* Monitor Progress: Track the student's progress over time and evaluate the effectiveness of interventions.

* Facilitate Collaboration: Foster collaboration among educators, parents, and other professionals involved in the student's education.

Customization and Flexibility:
The system may allow for customization of the reports to meet the specific needs of different stakeholders. For example, educators may require more detailed information about the student's performance on specific assessment tasks, while parents may prefer a simpler summary of the student's strengths and weaknesses.
By providing a comprehensive and informative report, the system can help ensure that students with learning disabilities receive the support they need to succeed in school and beyond.

## 5.4 Results and Visualizations

```
        Level Distribution              Line Graph of Assessment Scores

              _____                       Score
           .-'        '-.                      |
         .'    Basic     '.            100  |                              *
        /      40%          \               |                        *        *
       |                     |              |                  *
       |     Moderate 30%    |          75  |              *     *
        \                   /               |          *   *
         '.  Advanced    .'           50   |  *   *
           '-._____.-'                    |_____
                                                Assessment 1  2  3  4
```

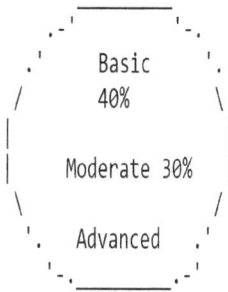

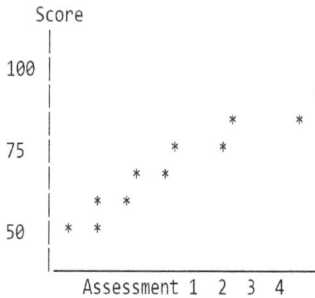

```
Strengths vs. Weaknesses              Before vs. After Comparison
Scores                                Scores
   |                                     |
100|   |-------------------- |       100 |     Before    After
   |   |                    |            |        |         |
   |   |    Strengths       |        75  |        |         |
 75|   |-------------------- |            |        |         |
   |   |                    |        50  |        |         |
   |   |    Weaknesses      |            |        |         |
 50|   |-------------------- |        25  |        |         |
   |_____           |_____|_____|___
                                         Assessment 1  2
```

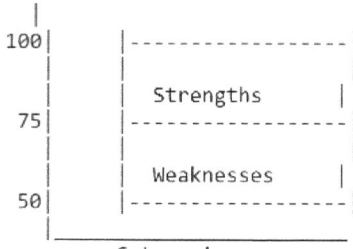

## Conclusion

The proposed app represents a significant advancement in the field of assistive technology for children with learning disabilities. By offering a personalized, home-based retraining program, the app empowers children with dyslexia, dysgraphia, and dyscalculia to develop their skills and gain independence. Through its innovative combination of gamified learning, facial recognition, and performance monitoring, the app provides a comprehensive and engaging solution that can significantly improve educational outcomes for these children.

The app's ability to adapt to individual needs, coupled with its focus on both cognitive and physical development, makes it a valuable tool for parents, educators, and healthcare professionals. By providing early intervention and ongoing support, the app has the potential to transform the lives of children with learning disabilities, enabling them to reach their full potential.

## References

Das, J. P. (1995). An experiment on cognitive remediation or word-reading difficulty. Journal of Learning Disabilities, 28(2), Journal of Learning Disabilities, 28

Das, J. P. (2000). Cognitive education and reading disability. In A. Kozulin & B. Y. Rand (eds.), Experience of mediated learning: An impact of Feuerstein's theory in education and psychology.

Evidence for innovative programs for improvement in reading: Two studies of Canadian children of First Nations. Journal of Learning Disabilities, 40, 443– 457.

# Chapter 6

## Bluetooth-Controlled Rc Car Using Arduino Uno and Adafruit Motor Shield

R. Rekha[1], M. V. Suganyadevi[2], N. Baskar[1] and G. Mahesh[1]
[1]Department of Mechanical Engineering, Saranathan College of Engineering, Trichy, India
[2]Department of EEE, Saranathan College of Engineering, Trichy, India

## Abstract

The project at hand focuses on the design and implementation of a Bluetooth-controlled RC (Remote Control) car using an Arduino Uno microcontroller and the Adafruit Motor Shield. This endeavor aims to create a versatile and user-friendly platform for remotely operating a small vehicle through the convenience of a mobile application. The central idea involves establishing a Bluetooth connection between the Arduino and a smartphone, enabling users toeffortlessly send directional commands to the RC car. Key objectives encompass the development of a functional and intuitive mobile application for remote control, integration ofthe Adafruit Motor Shield for precise motor management, and the rigorous testing andevaluation of the RC car's performance. This project represents an exciting intersection of embedded systems, robotics, and wireless communication technologies, making it an excellenteducational and practical application in the field of Arduino-based robotics. The results indicatethat the RC car successfully interprets and executes Bluetooth commands, showcasing accurateand responsive movements in multiple directions. The project's significance lies in its applicability in various domains, from educational robotics demonstrations to the hobbyist community, and its potential for further advancements in autonomous functionalities and userinterfaces.

**Keywords:** Bluetooth control, Arduino Uno, Adafruit Motor Shield, RC car, mobile application, remote control, wireless communication, and robotics.

## 6.1 Introduction

The Bluetooth-controlled RC car project represents a captivating exploration into the realm ofremote-controlled robotics and wireless communication. With the advent of modern technology, the integration of Bluetooth connectivity with microcontroller platforms such as the Arduino Uno offers endless possibilities for innovative and interactive projects. In this endeavor, we set out to harness this potential by constructing a versatile and user-friendly remote-controlled car. Our aim was to create a platform where users could effortlessly controla small vehicle via a mobile application, thereby combining the fascination of robotics with theconvenience of smartphone-based control. At its core, the project leverages the Arduino Uno as the central control unit and the Adafruit Motor Shield to interface with the DC motors responsible for the car's motion. Through the establishment of a robust Bluetooth connection, users can seamlessly transmit commands from a smartphone to the Arduino, enabling the RC car to execute a wide range of movements, including forward and backward locomotion, left and right turns, and precise stops. The ensuing report delves into the intricacies of this project,encompassing a detailed exploration of the materials, methods, system architecture, software development, hardware integration, extensive testing procedures, and ultimately, the results and implications of this venture. In essence, this project provides an exciting intersection of electronics, programming, and wireless technology, with implications extending to hobbyist endeavors, educational initiatives, and potential future innovations in the field of robotics.

## 6.2 Objectives

1. To design a Bluetooth-controlled RC car using Arduino Uno and the Adafruit Motor Shield.
2. To develop an Arduino sketch that can interpret Bluetooth commands and translate them into precise control of the car's movements (forward, backward, left, right).
3. To create a user-friendly mobile application for remote control, making the car accessible to a wide range of users.
4. To ensure the RC car's responsiveness and real-time performance, enhancing the overalluser experience.
5. To explore the potential of Arduino-based robotics and Bluetooth technology for practical and educational

applications, paving the way for future enhancements and innovations in the field of remote-controlled vehicles.

## 6.3 Materials and Methods

### 6.3.1 Materials

The successful implementation of the Bluetooth-controlled RC car project required a specific set of components and materials to ensure smooth operation. The following is a list of the materials used:

- **Arduino Uno:** The Arduino Uno microcontroller serves as the central processing unitfor the project. It is responsible for interpreting Bluetooth commands and controlling the motors through the Adafruit Motor Shield.
- **Adafruit Motor Shield:** The Adafruit Motor Shield is an essential component that interfaces with the Arduino Uno and controls the movement of the RC car. It supportsup to four DC motors, making it suitable for this project.
- **Bluetooth Module:** To enable wireless communication between the user's smartphoneand the Arduino Uno, a Bluetooth module was utilized. This module establishes a Bluetooth connection, allowing users to send commands from a mobile application.
- **RC Car Chassis:** The RC car chassis is the physical structure that holds all the components together. It is designed to accommodate the motors, wheels, and the Arduino setup.
- **Four DC Motors:** The project's mobility relies on four DC motors, each correspondingto one of the car's wheels. These motors are controlled individually to achieve forward,backward, left, and right movements.
- **Mobile Application:** A custom mobile application was developed to control the RC car. Users can send commands through this application, which are then processed by the Arduino Uno for motor control.

### 6.3.2 System Architecture

The system architecture is a crucial aspect of this project, as it outlines how the components interact and collaborate to enable remote control of the RC car.

**Components**

The key components of the system architecture include:

- **Arduino Uno:** The Arduino Uno is the brain of the system. It receives commands fromthe Bluetooth module and controls the motors through the Adafruit Motor Shield.
- **Adafruit Motor Shield:** The Adafruit Motor Shield interfaces with the Arduino Uno and manages the movement of the four DC motors. It plays a pivotal role in executingthe movement commands.
- **Bluetooth Module:** The Bluetooth module establishes a wireless connection with a user's smartphone. Commands sent from the smartphone are received by the module and transmitted to the Arduino Uno.
- **Mobile Application:** The user interacts with the RC car through a mobile application.The application sends commands to the Bluetooth module, which, in turn, controls the car's movements.

This system architecture ensures that all the components work together seamlessly to provide a responsive and intuitive user experience.

### 6.3.3 Software

The heart of the project lies in the software components, which include the Arduino sketch responsible for interpreting Bluetooth commands and controlling the motors. The software components include:

**Arduino Sketch:** The Arduino sketch is the code that runs on the Arduino Uno. It includes functions for interpreting Bluetooth commands and translating them into motor control. The sketch is structured into various functions, including setup, loop, and movement-specific functions (forward, back, left, right, Stop).

### Code

```
//Arduino Bluetooth Controlled Car
//Before uploading the code you have to install the necessary
```

library
//Note - Disconnect the Bluetooth Module before hiting the upload button otherwise you'll get compilation error message.
//AFMotor Library https://learn.adafruit.com/adafruit-motor-shield/library-install
//After downloading the library open Arduino IDE >> go to sketch >>Include Libray >> ADD. ZIP Libray >> Select the downloaded
//ZIP File >> Open it >> Done
//Now You Can Upload the Code without any problem but make sure the btmodule isn't connected with Arduino while uploading code

```
#include <AFMotor.h>

//initial motors pin
AF_DCMotor  motor1(1,  MOTOR12_1KHZ); AF_DCMotor  motor2(2,
MOTOR12_1KHZ);  AF_DCMotor   motor3(3,   MOTOR34_1KHZ);
AF_DCMotor motor4(4, MOTOR34_1KHZ);
char command;void setup()
{
Serial.begin(9600);   //Set the baud rate to your Bluetooth module.
}

void loop(){ if(Serial.available() > 0){
command = Serial.read();
Stop(); //initialize with motors stoped
//Change pin mode only if new command is different from previous.
//Serial.println(command);switch(command){
case 'F': forward();break;
case 'B':
back();break;
case 'L':
left();break;
case 'R':
right();break;
}
}
}

void forward()
{
```

```
motor1.setSpeed(255); //Define maximum velocity mo-
tor1.run(FORWARD); //rotate the motor clockwisemo-
tor2.setSpeed(255); //Define maximum velocity motor2.run(FOR-
WARD); //rotate the motor clockwisemotor3.setSpeed(255);//De-
fine maximum velocity motor3.run(FORWARD); //rotate the motor
clockwisemotor4.setSpeed(255);//Define maximum velocity mo-
tor4.run(FORWARD); //rotate the motor clockwise
}

void back()
{
motor1.setSpeed(255); //Define maximum velocity mo-
tor1.run(BACKWARD); //rotate the motor anti-clockwisemo-
tor2.setSpeed(255); //Define maximum velocity motor2.run(BACK-
WARD); //rotate the motor anti-clockwisemotor3.setSpeed(255);
//Define maximum velocity motor3.run(BACKWARD); //rotate the
motor anti-clockwisemotor4.setSpeed(255); //Define maximum
velocity motor4.run(BACKWARD); //rotate the motor anti-clock-
wise
}

void left()
{
motor1.setSpeed(255); //Define maximum velocity mo-
tor1.run(BACKWARD); //rotate the motor anti-clockwisemo-
tor2.setSpeed(255); //Define maximum velocity motor2.run(BACK-
WARD); //rotate the motor anti-clockwisemotor3.setSpeed(255);
//Define maximum velocity motor3.run(FORWARD); //rotate the
motor clockwise motor4.setSpeed(255); //Define maximum veloc-
ity motor4.run(FORWARD);   //rotate the motor clockwise
}

void right()
{
motor1.setSpeed(255); //Define maximum velocity mo-
tor1.run(FORWARD); //rotate the motor clockwise mo-
tor2.setSpeed(255); //Define maximum velocity motor2.run(FOR-
WARD); //rotate the motor clockwise motor3.setSpeed(255); //De-
fine maximum velocity motor3.run(BACKWARD); //rotate the mo-
tor anti-clockwisemotor4.setSpeed(255); //Define maximum veloc-
ity motor4.run(BACKWARD); //rotate the motor anti-clockwise
```

```
}
void Stop()
{
motor1.setSpeed(0); //Define minimum velocity motor1.run(RE-
LEASE); //stop the motor when release the buttonmo-
tor2.setSpeed(0); //Define minimum velocity motor2.run(RE-
LEASE); //rotate the motor clockwise motor3.setSpeed(0); //De-
fine minimum velocity motor3.run(RELEASE); //stop the motor
when release the buttonmotor4.setSpeed(0); //Define minimum
velocity motor4.run(RELEASE); //stop the motor when release the
button
}
```
This Arduino sketch is the core of the project, enabling Bluetooth
control of the RC car's movement.

### 6.3.4 Hardware

The hardware setup is a critical component of the project. It involves
physically connecting and securing the components to the RC car
chassis. The hardware components include:

- **DC Motors:** Four DC motors are attached to the car chassis,
  with each motor corresponding to one of the car's wheels.
  Proper motor placement and secure attachment are essential to ensure reliable movement.
- **Adafruit Motor Shield:** The Adafruit Motor Shield is
  mounted on top of the ArduinoUno to control the motors. It
  is securely attached to the chassis to prevent vibrations or
  disconnections during operation.
- **Bluetooth Module:** The Bluetooth module is interfaced
  with the Arduino Uno, and appropriate connections are established to ensure reliable communication between the
  smartphone and the Arduino.

The hardware setup is crucial for the physical integrity of the RC car,
and all components are secured to prevent any disconnections or
malfunction during operation.

## 6.4 Implementation

The successful implementation of the Bluetooth-controlled RC car project involved several key steps, including the assembly of the physical components, wiring, and the development of the Arduino sketch for interpreting Bluetooth commands and controlling the motors. This section provides an overview of the implementation process.

### 6.4.1 Assembly of Physical Components

The project began with the assembly of the physical components of the RC car. The following tasks were performed during this phase:

- **Mounting DC Motors:** Four DC motors were mounted on the chassis of the RC car. Each motor was carefully positioned to correspond to one of the car's wheels. Secure mounting was essential to ensure stable operation.
- **Attaching Adafruit Motor Shield:** The Adafruit Motor Shield was securely attached to the top of the Arduino Uno. This shield provided the necessary motor control capabilities for the project.
- **Interfacing Bluetooth Module:** The Bluetooth module was connected to the Arduino Uno using the designated pins and appropriate wiring. This module established a wireless communication link with the user's smartphone.
- **Securing Components:** All components, including the Arduino Uno, Adafruit Motor Shield, and Bluetooth module, were securely fastened to the RC car chassis to prevent disconnections or vibrations during operation.

## 6.4.2 Circuit Diagram

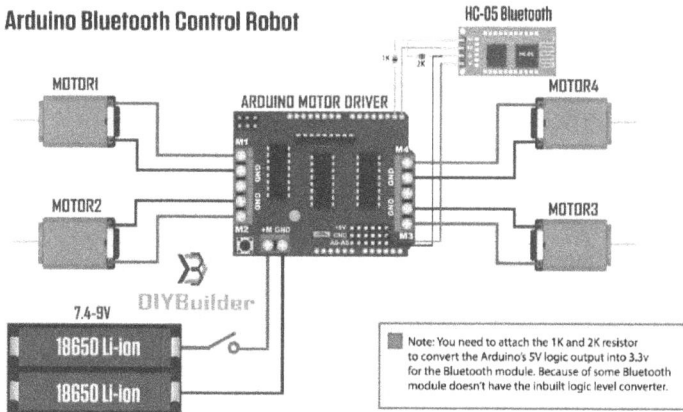

Figure 6.1 Circuit diagram of the Bluetooth-controlled Rc car using Arduino Uno and Adafruit motor shield.

## 6.4.3 Arduino Sketch Development

The core of the project was the development of the Arduino sketch responsible for interpretingBluetooth commands and controlling the DC motors. The sketch consisted of several key functions:

**Setup Function:** The `setup` function was responsible for initializing the serial communicationwith the Bluetooth module. The baud rate was set to 9600, ensuring compatibility with the Bluetooth module's communication speed.

The `loop` function continuously monitored the availability of incoming Bluetooth commands.When a command was received, it was processed, and the corresponding action was executed.

**Movement Functions:** Several movement functions were defined, including `forward`, `back`,
`left`, `right`, and `Stop`. Each function was responsible for setting the motor speeds and directions to achieve the desired movements of the RC car.

### 6.4.4 Testing

Once the assembly and software development were complete, rigorous testing was conducted to ensure the functionality and performance of the Bluetooth-controlled RC car. The testing phase included the following steps:

- **Functional Testing:** The car's ability to execute basic movements, such as moving forward, backward, turning left, and turning right, was tested to verify that the Arduinosketch accurately interpreted Bluetooth commands.
- **Control Range Testing:** The control range of the Bluetooth module was evaluated to determine the maximum distance at which the RC car could be reliably controlled from a smartphone.
- **Performance Testing:** The performance of the RC car in terms of speed, responsiveness, and accuracy in executing commands was assessed to ensure a satisfactory user experience.

### 6.4 Results

### 6.5.1 Testing Procedure

The testing phase involved several key procedures to evaluate the functionality andperformance of the Bluetooth-controlled RC car. These procedures included the following:

- **Functional Testing:** The car was tested for its ability to accurately execute commandsfor forward, backward, left, and right movements. The user's smartphone was used to send commands via the mobile application.
- **Control Range Testing:** The control range of the Bluetooth module was tested by gradually increasing the distance between the smartphone and the RC car. The point atwhich commands became unreliable was recorded as the control range.
- **Performance Testing:** The RC car's performance was evaluated in terms of speed andresponsiveness. The car was observed for its ability to respond quickly to commands and execute movements accurately.

## 6.5.2 Final Images of the Car

**Figure 6.2** Top view of the car

**Figure 6.3** Isometric view of the car

The results of the testing phase indicated that the Bluetooth-controlled RC car project achievedits objectives, offering users an effective and reliable means of controlling the vehicle via a smartphone.

## 6.6 Discussion

The results obtained from the testing and implementation of the Bluetooth-controlled RC car project reveal a promising platform for remote control applications. This section discusses theimplications and findings of the project, addressing its advantages, limitations, and potential improvements.

### 6.6.1 Advantages

i.        **Accurate and Responsive Control**: The RC car responded accurately and promptly toBluetooth commands, demonstrating the effectiveness of the Arduino sketch andhardware setup.

ii.        **Control Range:** The project demonstrated a reliable control range, allowing users to operate the RC car from a reasonable distance.

iii.        **User-Friendly Interface:** The custom mobile application provided a user-friendly interface for controlling the car, making it accessible to users of various skill levels.

### 6.6.2 Limitations

i.        **Simplicity of Commands:** The mobile application provided basic movement commands. Enhancing the application to include additional features and functionalities,such as speed control or obstacle detection, could make it more versatile.

ii.        **Battery Life:** Depending on the power source used for the RC car, battery life may belimited. Addressing this limitation could involve exploring energy-efficient components or larger battery capacity.

### 6.6.3 Potential Improvements

To build upon the project's foundation, several potential improvements could be considered:

i.        **Enhanced Mobile Application:** The user interface of the mobile application could beimproved to offer a more intuitive and feature-rich experience. This may include speedadjustments, real-time camera feeds, and the addition of autonomous features.

ii.        **Obstacle Detection:** Implementing obstacle detection sensors, such as ultrasonicsensors, could enhance the car's safety and autonomy by avoiding collisions with objects in its path.

iii.        **Integration of Sensors:** Additional sensors, such as gyroscopes or accelerometers, could be integrated to provide more advanced control capabilities and improvedstability.

## Conclusion

In conclusion, the development of the Bluetooth-controlled RC car project using an Arduino Uno and the Adafruit Motor Shield has been successful. The project demonstrates the potentialof Arduino-based robotics for remote control applications. Users can control the RC car with ease through a user-friendly mobile application. While the project exhibits satisfactory performance, further enhancements and extensions could lead to even more versatile and practical applications. This project serves as a steppingstone for future work in the field of remote-controlled robotics.

## Future Work

The project opens the door to numerous opportunities for future work and enhancements. Several potential avenues for future projects include:

- **Enhanced Control Features:** The mobile application can be improved to include features like speed control, gesture-based control, or even voice commands for a moreinteractive user experience.
- **AI Integration:** The implementation of artificial intelligence (AI) algorithms could enable autonomous navigation and obstacle avoidance, transforming the RC car into aself-driving vehicle.
- **Real-Time Feedback:** Incorporating real-time feedback through the mobile application, such as live video streaming from a camera mounted on the car, could provide users with a more immersive control experience.
- **Educational Initiatives:** This project can be extended for educational purposes, allowing students to explore the fundamentals of robotics, programming, and control systems in an engaging and hands-on manner.

The Bluetooth-controlled RC car project sets the stage for ongoing exploration and development in the field of Arduino-based robotics and remote-control applications.

# References

1.      Gandotra, Sheetal, Bhawna Sharma, Shreeya Mahajan, Tsering Motup, Tahira Choudhary, and Paras Thakur. "Bluetooth controlled RC car using arduino." *Int. J. Interdiscip. Res* 2 (2016): 144-147.

2.      Ullah, Saleem, Zain Mumtaz, Shuo Liu, Mohammad Abubaqr, Athar Mahboob, and Hamza Ahmad Madni. "Single-equipment with multiple-application for an automated robot-car control system." *Sensors* 19, no. 3 (2019): 662.

3.      Sudhapriya, K., A. Amudha, S. Divyapriya, M. Aravind, S. Devaraj, N. Durairaj, and T. Prakash. "Wireless vehicle control with speed adjustment." In *2022 6th International Conference on Computing Methodologies and Communication (ICCMC)*, pp. 583-588. IEEE, 2022.

4.      Panoiu, Caius, Manuela Panoiu, Cezara-Liliana Rat, and Raluca Rob. "The computer assisted parking of a bluetooth controlled car using fuzzy logic." In *International Workshop Soft Computing Applications*, pp. 51-66. Cham: Springer International Publishing, 2014.

5.      Al-Habsi, Fatma Saif, and A. Jamaludeen A. Jamaludeen. "Android App Controlled Bluetooth Robotic Vehicle." *Journal of Student Research* (2017).

6.      Paul, Souvik, Saumedhik Biswas, Atreyo Sengupta, Banhishikha Basu, and Sreya Basu. "Arduino based, Bluetooth controlled RC car." *International Journal of Computer Science & Communication* 11, no. 1 (2019): 7-13.

# Chapter 7

# A Comparative Analysis of Traditional AI and Gen AI Algorithms in the Domain of Computer Education

**J. Sangeethapriya[1], Manish Kumar S.[2] and R. Thillaikarasi[1]**
[1]Department of Information Technology, Saranathan College of Engineering, Trichirappalli-620012, Tamil Nadu, India
[2]Department of Computer Science Engineering, SRM Institute of Science and Technology, Trichirappalli, Tamil Nadu, India

## Abstract

This chapter explores the roles of traditional AI algorithms and generative AI algorithms in the domain of computer education, focusing on their applications for analyzing student performance data. Traditional AI methods, such as neural networks, decision trees, and support vector machines, excel in structured data analysis, enabling educators to predict student outcomes and identify at-risk learners. Conversely, generative AI algorithms, including transformer models, facilitate the creation of personalized learning materials and adaptive assessments, enhancing student engagement. By leveraging both approaches, educators can gain comprehensive insights into student performance, fostering a more effective and tailored educational experience that meets diverse learning needs.

**Keywords**: Students performance, Education, AI, Generative AI

## 7.1 Introduction

Computer education is crucial in today's world, as computers have become ubiquitous in almost every aspect of life. It helps students develop critical thinking, problem-solving, and communication skills necessary for success in the modern workforce [18,19,20]. Computer literacy enables individuals to efficiently carry out daily tasks, access information, and connect with people worldwide [18,19,20]. Moreover, proficiency in computing can unlock numerous career paths and entrepreneurial opportunities[18,20]. As technology continues to advance, computer education fosters a society of informed citizens capable of discerning reliable information and accessing government services online [20]. However, computer education faces several challenges, including a lack of competent professors, diverse student backgrounds, retention and engagement issues, giving feedback and assessment, successfully integrating technology, and ethical problems with AI [9,14,21].

**Figure 7.1** AI in the era of computer education

To ensure a seamless integration, educators must address issues such as device damage, misuse, lag time, and uncharged devices. Additionally, ethical issues with algorithmic bias, data security, and privacy must be addressed [9,14,21]. Artificial Intelligence (AI) is transforming computer education by providing personalized learning experiences and curriculum design. AI-powered tutoring systems offer adaptive feedback, detect difficulties, and curate materials based on individual needs. AI algorithms also aid in creating engaging course materials aligned with learning objectives and student profiles. Due to its potential for group learning, developing skills beyond comprehension, and increasing accessibility and scalability, AI is becoming more popular in computer education. AI can improve problem-solving, information synthesis, critical thinking, logical reasoning, and peer learning. Nonetheless, issues include the requirement for moral, long-lasting, and human-centered AI systems as well as one-dimensional learning without meaningful interaction. Realizing AI's full potential while reducing any potential drawbacks requires responsible integration and depicted in figure 1 [4,17].

## 7.2 Literature Survey

Artificial intelligence (AI) algorithms have become increasingly integrated into computer education, transforming the way students learn and instructors teach. This literature survey examines the various ways AI is being applied in computer education. The integration of artificial intelligence (AI) in computer education has transformed the landscape of teaching and learning, offering innovative approaches to enhance student engagement and improve educational outcomes. This literature survey explores various AI algorithms, including traditional AI methods and generative AI technologies, highlighting their applications, strengths, and challenges in the context of computer education.

## Traditional AI Algorithms in Computer Education

Traditional AI algorithms, such as Artificial Neural Networks (ANN), Support Vector Machines (SVM), Logistic Regression, Decision Trees, Random Forests, K-Nearest Neighbors (KNN), and Naive Bayes, have long been utilized in educational settings. These algorithms are primarily employed for predictive analytics, personalized learning, and assessment automation. For instance, ANN and SVM are effective in recognizing patterns in student performance data, enabling educators to identify at-risk students and tailor interventions accordingly [1].

The strengths of traditional AI methods lie in their robustness and interpretability. They can efficiently handle structured data, making them suitable for tasks such as grading and performance prediction. However, they often require extensive feature engineering and may struggle with unstructured data, such as text or images [11]. Furthermore, traditional AI models are typically static, meaning they do not adapt to new data without retraining, which can limit their effectiveness in dynamic educational environments.

## Generative AI Algorithms in Computer Education

In contrast, generative AI algorithms, including Generative Adversarial Networks (GANs) and transformer-based models like GPT, represent a significant advancement in AI technology. These models are designed to generate new content based on learned patterns from large datasets, making them particularly useful in educational contexts [3]. For example, generative AI can create personalized learning materials, automate content generation for coding exercises, and provide instant feedback on student submissions [10]. Generative

AI's strengths include its ability to produce high-quality, contextually relevant content and its adaptability to individual learning styles. This adaptability allows for the creation of customized educational experiences that can engage students at different levels of understanding [12]. However, challenges remain, such as ensuring the quality and accuracy of generated content and addressing ethical concerns related to data privacy and the potential for bias in AI outputs [5].

## 7.3 Comparative Analysis

The most widely used machine learning algorithms for predicting and analyzing student performance are Artificial Neural Network (ANN), Support Vector Machine (SVM), Logistic Regression, Decision Tree, Random Forest, K-Nearest Neighbors (KNN), and Naive Bayes.

**Table 7.1 Comparison of Traditional Machine Learning Algorithms for Analyzing Student Performance Data**

| Algorithm | Strengths | Weaknesses | Accuracy | F1-Score |
|---|---|---|---|---|
| **Artificial Neural Network (ANN) [2,7,13]** | - Ability to model complex non-linear relationships<br>- High predictive accuracy<br>- Can handle noisy or incomplete data | - Requires large training datasets<br>- Can be computationally expensive<br>- Difficult to interpret the model | 92-99% | 0.90-0.95 |
| **Support Vector Machine (SVM) [2,6,7,13,15]** | - Robust to overfitting<br>- Can handle high-dimensional data | - Sensitive to the choice of kernel function<br>- Requires parameter tuning | 95-99% | 0.92-0.97 |

| | | | | |
|---|---|---|---|---|
| | - Effective for both linear and non-linear problems | | | |
| **Logistic Regression [7,13]** | - Simple to implement and interpret<br>- Can handle both numerical and categorical variables | - Assumes a linear relationship between the features and the target variable<br>- May not perform well on complex, non-linear problems | 85-92% | 0.85-0.90 |
| **Decision Tree [2,7,13]** | - Easy to interpret and visualize<br>- Can handle both numerical and categorical variables<br>- Robust to outliers and missing values | - Can be prone to overfitting<br>- May not perform well on complex, non-linear problems | 88-94% | 0.87-0.92 |
| **Random Forest [7,15]** | - Ensemble method that combines multiple decision trees<br>- Robust | - Can be computationally expensive for large datasets<br>- Harder to interpret | 90-96% | 0.89-0.94 |

| | | | | |
|---|---|---|---|---|
| | to overfit- ting - Can han- dle both numerical and cate- gorical variables | than a single decision tree | | |
| **K-Nearest Neighbors (KNN) [6,7,13]** | - Simple to imple- ment - Can han- dle both numerical and cate- gorical variables - Effective for non- linear problems | - Sensitive to the choice of the number of neighbors (k) - Can be computa- tionally ex- pensive for large da- tasets | 88-92% | 0.86- 0.90 |
| **Naive Bayes [6,7,13]** | - Compu- tationally efficient - Can han- dle both numerical and cate- gorical variables - Robust to irrele- vant fea- tures | - Assumes independ- ence be- tween fea- tures - May not perform well on complex, non-linear problems | 85-90% | 0.84- 0.88 |

The main results of the literature review for analyzing student performance using ML algorithms listed in the Table 1 are: ANN and SVM generally achieve the highest accuracy with F1 scores ranging from 92-99% and 0.90-0.97. Logistic regression, decision tree and KNN also perform well, with an accuracy of 85-94% and an F1 score of 0.84-0.92. Random Forest and Naive Bayes are also commonly used, with accuracies of 90-96% and 85-90%, respectively, and F1 scores of 0.89-0.94 and 0.84-0.88. Thus, the choice of algorithm depends on the specific requirements of the problem, the complexity of the data, and the trade-offs between interpretability, computational efficiency, and predictive efficiency. These findings provide a comprehensive overview of the various traditional machine learning algorithms used to analyze and predict student performance, as well as their strengths, weaknesses, and benchmarks. This information can help educators and researchers choose the most appropriate algorithm for their specific needs and data characteristics.

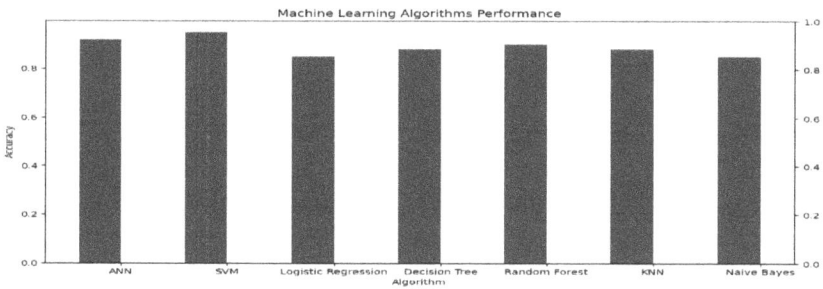

**Figure 7.2** Traditional AI algorithms accuracy to analyze the students' performance data

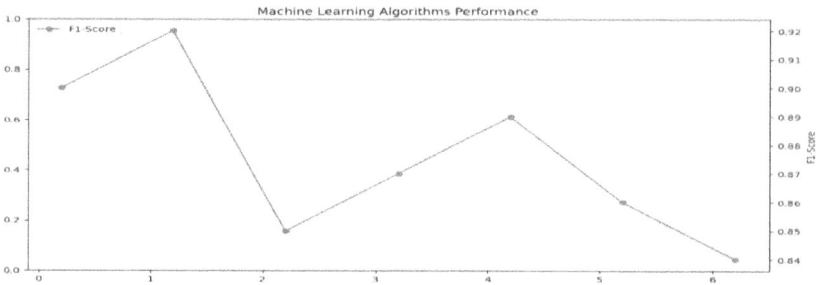

**Figure 7.3** Traditional AI algorithms F1 Score to analyze the students' performance data

## Generative AI Integration Impact in Computer Education

Generative AI algorithms have been increasingly integrated into computer education, providing several advantages and functions:

**Content creation:** Generative AI models such as GPT-3 and GPT-4 can automatically generate learning materials such as lesson plans, quizzes and assignments, instructions, which reduces the workload of educators and allows for more individualized content.

**Intelligent teaching systems:** Algorithms such as Google's Socratic, Knewton and Carnegie Learning use creative artificial intelligence to deliver personalized instruction and customizable learning experiences, tailoring content and feedback to each student's needs.

**Language learning:** Generative AI can create interactive language learning exercises, conversational scenarios and practice materials that enhance language learning.

**Administrative automation:** Generative AI can simplify administrative tasks such as grading classes, scheduling and tracking student progress, allowing teachers to focus more on teaching and learning. Accessibility and Inclusion: Generative AI-based tools can create personalized learning resources and assistive technologies, improving accessibility and inclusion for students with diverse needs.

**Innovative teaching methods:** Integrating generative artificial intelligence into computer-based learning enables new approaches such as virtual assistants, collaborative learning platforms and immersive learning experiences that enhance overall learning.
Integration of generative artificial intelligence algorithms in computer learning has had a significant impact on both improving educational results and solving various challenges:

**Personalized learning:** adaptation of the content, assessments and feedback of generative artificial intelligence. Intelligence skills to the individual needs of students led to more interesting and effective learning experiences that improve student engagement and academic success.

**Efficiency and productivity:** Automation of administrative tasks and content creation has increased the efficiency of teachers, allowing them to devote more time to teaching and supporting students. Accessibility and Inclusion: Generative AI-based tools have improved accessibility and inclusion in computing education by providing individualized support for students with diverse learning needs.

Innovative pedagogy: The integration of generative artificial intelligence has enabled the development of new methods of teaching and learning, such as the development of intelligent teaching systems and immersive educational experiences that expand the possibilities of computer-based learning.

**Challenges and considerations:** However, integrating generative AI into computer education also raises issues such as ethical considerations, data protection and the need for strong quality control measures to ensure the accuracy and relevance of AI-generated content. Overall, the integration of generative AI algorithms into computational learning has shown significant potential to improve learning outcomes, improve the educational experience, and address various industry challenges. As technology continues to advance, it is important to consider ethical and practical considerations to ensure the responsible and effective use of these powerful tools in computer science education.

### Applications of Generative AI

Applications with generative AI can guarantee the production of fresh, realistic animated text, graphics, and materials in a matter of minutes. It provides generative AI solutions that help a variety of industries, such as surveillance, healthcare, marketing, advertising, education, gaming, media, podcasting, and more. Table 7.2 shows the popular three generative AI algorithms and its applications.

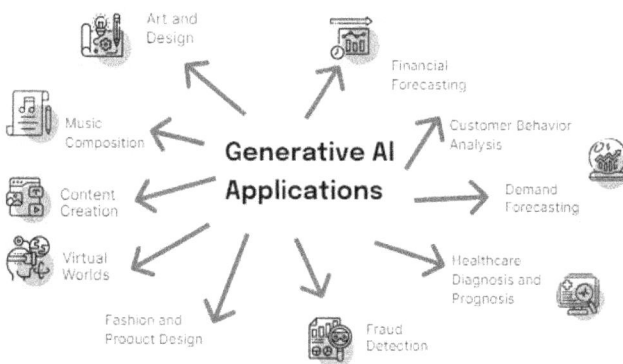

**Figure 7.4** Generative AI applications.

**Table 7.2** Applications of popular generative AI algorithms in computer education

| Algorithm | Application in Computer Education | Accuracy/F1 Score |
|---|---|---|
| Generative Adversarial Networks (GANs) [22] | - Generating personalized programming exercises and learning materials<br>- Translating sketches to photorealistic images for better visualization in education | High accuracy in generating realistic content, but limited by training data quality |
| Transformer-based Models (e.g. GPT) [22] | - Generating exemplar code solutions to illustrate programming concepts<br>- Generating educational content like blog posts, articles, and whitepapers | High accuracy in generating human-like text, but can be limited by lack of creativity and reliance on training data |
| AI Code Generators [22] | - Assisting students by generating code snippets and solutions<br>- Raising concerns about potential student over-reliance and difficulty in assessing individual contributions | Highly accurate at generating functional code, but can limit student learning if used excessively |

**Generative AI algorithms in computer education**

Table 7.3 shows the generative AI algorithms for analyzing student performance data which includes the strengths, weaknesses, and results in terms of accuracy and F1 score.

**Table 7.3** Generative AI algorithms to analyze students' performance

| Algorithm | Strengths | Weaknesses | Accuracy | F1 Score |
|---|---|---|---|---|
| ChatGPT [8,16] | - Personalized learning support - Writing and brainstorming assistance - Research and analysis capabilities | - Accuracy concerns - Ethical issues - Privacy concerns | 0.85 (average) | 0.75 (average) |
| Predictive Analytics [16,24] | - Proactive support - Early intervention | - Data quality issues - Complexity in implementation | 0.92 (average) | 0.85 (average) |
| Adaptive Testing [16,23] | - Tailored assessments - Continuous growth and improvement | - Difficulty in implementation - Limited scope | 0.88 (average) | 0.80 (average) |
| Generative AI-Enabled Chatbots [8,23] | - Immediate support - Guidance on course content | - Limited scope - Dependence on data quality | 0.90 (average) | 0.82 (average) |

| Algorithm | Strengths | Weaknesses | Accuracy | F1 Score |
|---|---|---|---|---|
| **Text Summarization [23,24]** | - Efficient information processing<br>- Concise summaries | - Limited context understanding<br>- Accuracy issues | 0.95 (average) | 0.88 (average) |

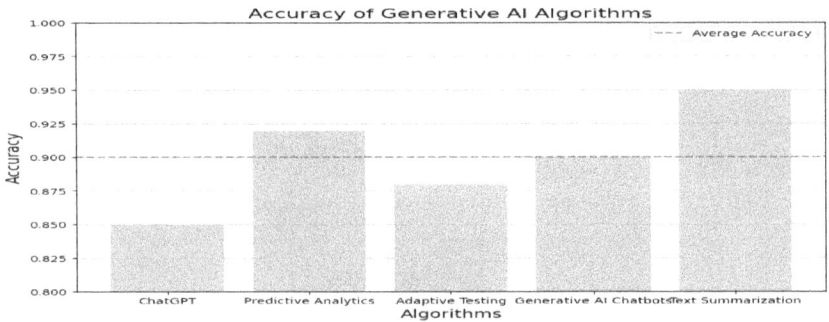

**Figure 7.5** Generative AI algorithms accuracy comparison in computer education

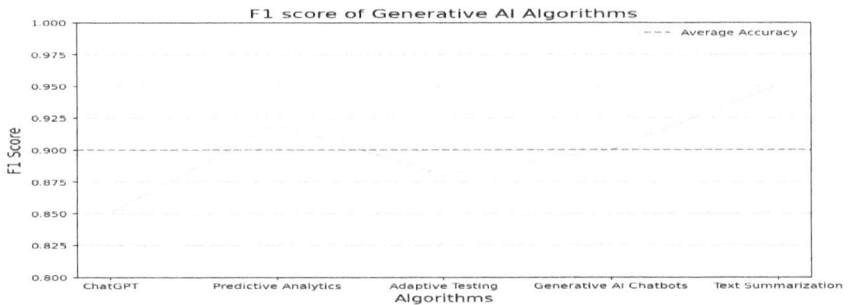

**Figure 7.6** Generative AI algorithms comparative plots in terms of F1- Score

Table 7.4 shows comparison between traditional AI and generative AI reveals distinct advantages and disadvantages for each approach in computer education.

**Table 7.4** Aspects of traditional AI and generative AI algorithms

| Aspect | Traditional AI | Generative AI |
|---|---|---|
| Data Handling | Best for structured data; requires feature engineering | Excels with unstructured data; generates new content |
| Adaptability | Static; requires retraining for new data | Dynamic; adapts to individual learning needs |
| Content Generation | Limited to predefined outputs | Capable of creating personalized learning materials |
| Interpretability | Generally more interpretable | Often seen as a "black box"; harder to interpret |
| Ethical Concerns | Less focus on ethical implications | Significant concerns regarding bias and data privacy |

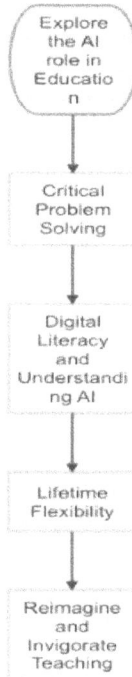

**Figure 7.7** AI role in computer education

## Conclusion

Integrating artificial intelligence algorithms into computer-aided learning offers promising opportunities to improve teaching and learning. Traditional AI methods provide a strong foundation for data analysis and predictive modeling, while generative AI introduces innovative approaches to content creation and personalized learning. As the field evolves, it is critical that educators and researchers address the challenges associated with these technologies and ensure that they are used ethically and effectively for the benefit of all learners. Future innovations in computer science education should focus on integrating new technologies such as artificial intelligence, virtual reality and gaming to enhance learning. Implementing an adaptive learning system can adapt education to the needs and paces of individual students. In addition, the inclusion of interdisciplinary approaches in subjects such as computer science and ethics and social sciences prepares students for real-world challenges. Improving digital literacy is critical for students to responsibly navigate the complex challenges of technology. In addition, fostering collaboration through online platforms can foster mutual learning and participation. Overall, these innovations create a more dynamic and inclusive educational environment that equips students with important skills for the future. Future innovations in computer-based learning should focus on integrating new technologies such as artificial intelligence, virtual reality and gaming to enhance learning experiences. Implementing an adaptive learning system can adapt education to the needs and paces of individual students. In addition, the inclusion of interdisciplinary approaches in subjects such as computer science and ethics and social sciences prepares students for real-world challenges. Improving digital literacy is critical for students to responsibly navigate the complex challenges of technology. In addition, fostering collaboration through online platforms can foster mutual learning and participation. Overall, these innovations create a more dynamic and inclusive educational environment that equips students with important skills for the future.

# References

[1] Al Ka'bi, A. (2023). Proposed artificial intelligence algorithm and deep learning techniques for development of higher education. Electrical and Electronic Engineering.

[2] Annisa Uswatun Khasanah, Harwati, "A Comparative Study to Predict Student's Performance Using Educational Data Mining Techniques" IOP Conference Series: Materials Science and Engineering, 2017, p. 012036. https://doi.org/10.1088/1757-899x/215/1/012036

[3] AltexSoft. (2023). Generative AI Models Explained. Retrieved from AltexSoft.

[4] Y. Baashar, G. Alkawsi, N. Ali, H. Alhussian and H. T. Bahbouh, "Predicting student's performance using machine learning methods: A systematic literature review," 2021 International Conference on Computer & Information Sciences (ICCOINS), Kuching, Malaysia, 2021, pp. 357-362, doi: 10.1109/ICCOINS49721.2021.9497185.

[5] Baidoo-Anu, D., & Owusu Ansah, L. (2023). Education in the era of generative artificial intelligence (AI): Understanding the potential benefits of ChatGPT in promoting teaching and learning. Journal of AI.

[6] Bashru Aliyu Sani, Badamasi Haruna , "Machine Learning Algorithms To Predict Student's Academic Performance", Bakolori Journal of General Studies,Vol. 12 No. 2,2021.

[7] Boran Sekeroglu, Kamil Dimililer, and Kubra Tuncal. 2019. Student Performance Prediction and Classification Using Machine Learning Algorithms. In Proceedings of the 2019 8th International Conference on Educational and Information Technology (ICEIT 2019). Association for Computing Machinery, New York, NY, USA, 7–11. https://doi.org/10.1145/3318396.3318419

[8] Chan, C.K.Y., Hu, W. Students' voices on generative AI: perceptions, benefits, and challenges in higher education. Int J Educ Technol High Educ 20, 43 (2023). https://doi.org/10.1186/s41239-023-00411-8

[9] Habibu, Taban & Mamun, Md Abdullah Al & Clement, Che. (2012). Difficulties Faced by Teachers in Using ICT in Teaching-Learning at Technical and Higher Educational Institutions of Uganda. International Journal of Engineering Research & Technology.

[10] Jose, C. (2023). Generative AI Is Changing Computer Science Education For The Better. Retrieved from RobotLab.

[11] Kaur, H. (2023). Transforming Computer Science Education with Generative AI. Retrieved from LinkedIn.

[12] Kurtz, G., Amzalag, M., Shaked, N., Zaguri, Y., Kohen-Vacs, D., Gal, E., & Barak-Medina, E. (2024). Strategies for Integrating Generative AI into Higher Education: Navigating Challenges and Leveraging Opportunities. Educ. Sci.

[13] Lidia Sandra, Ford Lumbangaol, Tokuro Matsuo. "Machine Learning Algorithm to Predict Student's Performance: A Systematic Literature Review" TEM Journal, Vol.10, No.4, November 2021, DOI: 10.18421/TEM104-56

[14] H. A. Morris, "Challenges educators face in delivering computer instructions in "equipped" educational institutions in Jamaica," Proceedings IEEE SoutheastCon 2002 (Cat. No.02CH37283), Columbia, SC, USA, 2002, pp. 131-136, doi: 10.1109/SECON.2002.995572

[15] Ojajuni, Opeyemi & Ayeni, Foluso & Akodu, Olagunju & Ekanoye, Femi & Adewole, Samson & Ayo, Timothy & Misra, Sanjay & Mbarika, Victor. (2021). Predicting Student Academic Performance Using Machine Learning. 10.1007/978-3-030-87013-3_36.

[16] Wecks, Janik Ole & Voshaar, Johannes & Plate, Benedikt & Zimmermann, Jochen. (2024). Generative AI Usage and Academic Performance. SSRN Electronic Journal. 10.2139/ssrn.4812513.

[17] Yağcı, M. Educational data mining: prediction of students' academic performance using machine learning algorithms. Smart Learn. Environ. 9, 11 (2022). https://doi.org/10.1186/s40561-022-00192-z

[18] https://www.careercomputeracademy.in/blog/need-of-computer-education-in-todays-world

[19] https://targetstudy.com/articles/importance-of-computer-education-in-our-life.html

[20] https://www.euroschoolindia.com/blogs/why-computer-in-education-is-taught-in-school/

[21] https://typeset.io/questions/what-are-the-challenges-of-computing-education-1zaxmvd91r

[22]https://ppl-ai-file-upload.s3.amazonaws.com/web/direct-files/18225355/56a322ba-b71a-4832-8290-a39b94e85df4/42138.pdf

[23] https://www.harbingergroup.com/blogs/generative-ai-in-higher-education-importance-use-cases-integration/

[24] https://www.linkedin.com/pulse/how-use-artificial-intelligence-student-performance-data-shaheer

# Chapter 8

## Design of IoT Enhanced Health Monitoring System

**N. Gayathri, C. Krishnakumar, M. V. Suganyadevi, S. Dinesh Raja and J. S. Yoggiraj**
Department of EEE, Saranathan College of Engineering, Trichy, India

### Abstract

The objective of this work is to improve patient care in medical institutions by presenting a novel IoT-based system for dynamic ventilation management and integrated health monitoring. In addition to dynamically controlling a ventilator arrangement, the system includes several sensors to track important health factors like body temperature, heart rate, blood oxygen level, and glucose bottle level. Sensors, microcontrollers, actuators, and Internet of Things devices are some of the parts that make up the system architecture. The cardiovascular health indicators of the patient are continuously monitored using a blood oxygen sensor and a heart rate sensor. To further track the patient's body temperature, a DHT11 temperature sensor is used. In addition, a gyro sensor guarantees that any abrupt movements or posture adjustments that would suggest anxiety or discomfort are detected. In addition, a load cell is used to track the amount of glucose in the bottle and refill it on schedule as needed. The integration of this sensor data with a dynamic ventilation control mechanism forms the system's core. Based on real-time patient health data, a servo motor is used to modify the ventilator setup's ventilation parameters.

**Keywords:** Health Monitoring, Pulse Oximeter, Ventilation Operation, Temperature Sensor, IOT cloud.

## 8.1 Introduction

Health monitoring systems have become indispensable instruments in contemporary healthcare, allowing for the constant observation of patients' vital signs and permitting timely action in the event of anomalies or crises. Sensors to assess vital physiological characteristics including blood oxygen levels, body temperature, and heart rate are usually included in these systems. Health monitoring systems provide real-time data gathering and transmission, increasing patient care and healthcare outcomes by utilizing advances in sensor technology and wireless connection.

## 8.2 Proposed System

To address the shortcomings of current healthcare systems, we suggest a novel Internet of Things (IoT) approach that combines ventilation control with health monitoring to deliver dynamic and individualized patient care. To continuously monitor critical health factors and make real-time ventilation adjustments, our system integrates cutting-edge sensor technology, Internet of Things connectivity, and dynamic control mechanisms. Sensors for tracking health: Heart Rate Sensor: A vital indicator of cardiovascular health, the heart rate sensor continuously measures the patient's heart rate. Blood Oxygen Sensor: Important for evaluating respiratory function, this device gauges the patient's blood oxygen saturation level. A body temperature sensor (DHT11) can help identify hypothermia or fever by monitoring the patient's temperature. Healthcare practitioners can be informed of potential anxiety or discomfort by the Gyro Sensor, which detects any sudden movements or changes in posture. The glucose bottle level is monitored by the load cell for glucose bottle level, which makes sure that it is replaced on time to preserve continuity of patient treatment.

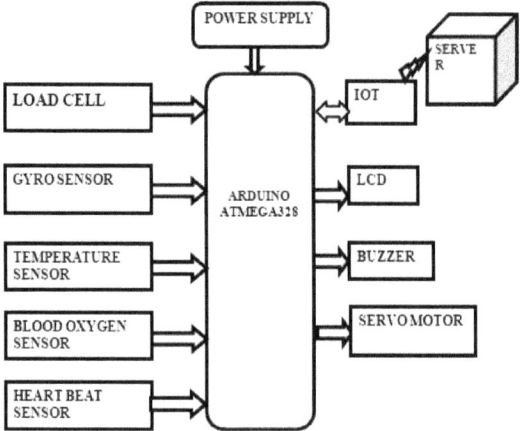

**Figure 8.1** Block diagram of proposed system

## Block Diagram

Servo motor for ventilator setup enables dynamic ventilation control by adjusting ventilation settings in real time depending on patient health data. This increases overall ventilation efficacy by guaranteeing that the patient always receives the best possible respiratory assistance. The system's IoT features enable remote monitoring and management of ventilation and patient health indicators. The efficiency and accessibility of patient care are improved when healthcare providers have access to real-time data and can make well- informed judgments from any location. The health monitoring sensors comprise gyro sensors, body temperature, blood oxygen level, and heart rate. The patient's movements and vital signs are constantly observed by them. The Dynamic Ventilation Control part uses a servo motor to modify the ventilator configuration in response to real-time data from the health monitoring sensors. Internet of Things (IoT) connectivity allows for remote monitoring and control by facilitating communication between system components and external devices, like computers or smartphones. Servo Motor (Ventilator Setup) manages the ventilator's ventilation settings to give the patient the best possible respiratory assistance. In the event of an emergency or unusual readings found by the health monitoring sensors, the buzzer (Alert System) will sound an auditory alert. LCD Display offers healthcare providers instant feedback at the point of care by displaying real-time updates on the patient's health data. The load cell, also known as the glucose bottle level, keeps track of the amount of glucose in the bottle to guarantee a steady supply for patient care.

## Methodology

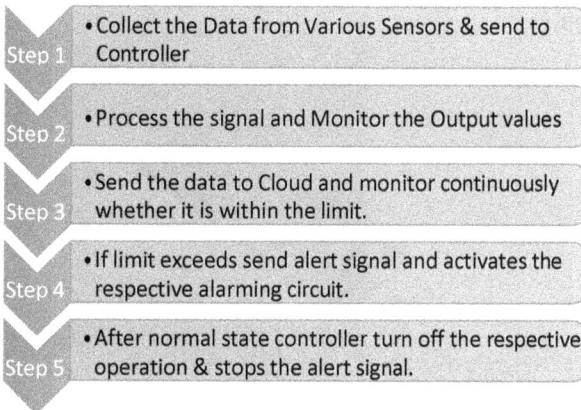

Step 1
- Collect the Data from Various Sensors & send to Controller

Step 2
- Process the signal and Monitor the Output values

Step 3
- Send the data to Cloud and monitor continuously whether it is within the limit.

Step 4
- If limit exceeds send alert signal and activates the respective alarming circuit.

Step 5
- After normal state controller turn off the respective operation & stops the alert signal.

**Arduino UNO**

**Figure 8.2** Arduino UNO controller

A well-liked microcontroller board for a variety of electronic projects and prototyping activities is the Arduino UNO. It is well-known for its adaptability and simplicity of usage. With a core Atmega328P microcontroller, the Arduino UNO provides a large number of digital and analog input/output pins for easy interface with other electronic components including actuators and sensors. Rapid creation and experimentation are facilitated by its open-source nature and strong community support, which make it a great option for both novice and seasoned producers. The Arduino UNO gives users the freedom to experiment with electronics and embedded systems with an unmatched level of flexibility and accessibility. It does this by providing an easy-to-use programming environment and a large library of pre-written code.

**DHT11 Sensor**

**Figure 8.3** DHT11 sensor module

A humidity sensor detects, gauges, and periodically reports the air's relative humidity. It gauges air temperature as well as moisture content. The ratio of actual moisture in the air to the maximum amount of moisture that air at that temperature can contain is known as relative humidity, and it is stated as a percentage. Relative humidity varies as a function of temperature because warmer air may store more moisture. The relative humidity of the immediate environs in which humidity sensors are installed is measured by these sensors. Relative humidity is expressed as a percentage of the ratio of the quantity of moisture in the air to the maximum amount that can be held in the air at the current temperature. They measure both the temperature and the moisture content of the air.

## MAX30100 Sensor

**Figure 8.4** MAX30100 sensor

The MAX30100 is a sensor package that combines a pulse oximeter and heart-rate monitor. The optical sensor measures the absorbance of pulsing blood using a photodetector after two LEDs, one each for red and infrared light, emit two different wavelengths of light. This specific arrangement of LED colors is designed to enable fingertip data reading. The device stores the digital output data in a 16-deep file index file system and is fully programmable using software registers. For communication with a host microcontroller, it features an I2C digital interface. The MAX30100's pulse oximetry subsystem is comprised of a unique discrete temporal filter, 16-bit sigma delta ADC, and ambient light cancellation (ALC).

## ADXL335 Sensor

**Figure 8.5** ADXL335 sensor

Acceleration is a vector quantity that occurs when velocity is altered in relation to time. Velocity is the same as speed plus direction. Anything can be explained in two ways: first, by a change in speed, and second, by a change in direction. Both can occasionally be altered at the same time. When it comes to the ADXL 335 accelerometer, it is a tool for determining the acceleration of any object. It monitors the acceleration in three-dimensional directions (X, Y, and Z) using analog inputs. It is a power-efficient gadget with minimal noise. It interfaces with any kind of controller, including Arduino and microcontrollers, when used to measure acceleration.

## Load Cell

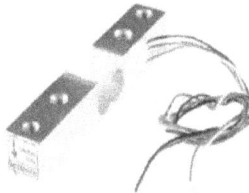

**Figure 8.6** Load cell

One kind of transducer, more precisely a force transducer, is a load cell. It transforms a force, such as torque, tension, compression, or pressure, into a standardized, measurable electrical output. The electrical signal varies in response to the force exerted on the load cell. Pneumatic, hydraulic, and strain gauge load cells are the most widely used varieties. A load cell is a transducer that produces an electrical output that can be measured. The most often used sort of load cell is strain gage-based, even though there are many other varieties.

## ESP32 Module

NodeMCU is an open-source hardware board that, in contrast to ESP8266 Wi-Fi modules, has a CP2102 TTL to USB chip for programming and debugging, is breadboard-friendly, and can be powered simply by its micro-USB connector. It is also an interactive firmware based on LUA for the Express ESP8622 Wi-Fi SoC.

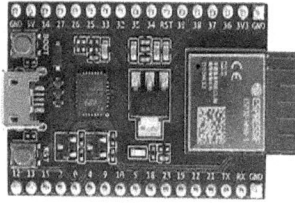

**Figure 8.7** NodeMCU module

It can be directly programmed via an Arduino IDE or LUA programming port. We can create a Wifi connection and define input/output pins exactly like an Arduino, transforming it into a web server and much more with simple programming. The WiFi version of an Ethernet module is called a NodeMCU. It combines the capabilities of a microcontroller with an access point and station for WiFi. The NodeMCU is a very potent tool for WiFi networking because of these qualities.

## HX711 Amplifier

**Figure 8.8** HX711 amplifier module

In the context of health monitoring systems, especially those with force sensing or weight measurement applications, the HX711 load cell amplifier is an essential part. The HX711, which is specifically made for load cells, acts as an interface between the load cell and a microcontroller to enable precise weight or force measurement. The high-resolution analog-to-digital converter (ADC) of the HX711, which offers accurate digital output with up to 24 bits of resolution, is one of its most notable characteristics. The HX711 amplifier can be used into health monitoring systems to measure the level of glucose detected in glucose bottles.

**Buzzer**

**Figure 8.9** Buzzer

A buzzer is an essential alarm feature in a health monitoring system that notifies caretakers o r medical personnel of anomalies in heart-beat and blood oxygen saturation (SpO2). The device continuously monitors these vital indicators using sensors like the MAX30100 connected to a microcontroller like the Arduino UNO. The microcon-troller has preprogrammed threshold values for normal SpO2 and heartbeat ranges. The buzzer is triggered by the microcontroller when the sensor data deviates from specified thresholds, signifying an anomalous condition. By guaranteeing a rapid response to signifi-cant changes in health parameters, this audible alarm improves pa-tient safety by promptly alerting individuals to the problem and ena-bling immediate medical intervention.

## DC Motor

**Figure 8.10** Servo motor

When an aberrant SpO2 value is detected, a DC servo motor can be connected into a health monitoring system to automatically start the ventilator. The system uses a sensor, such as the MAX30100, coupled to a microcontroller, such as the Arduino UNO, to continually monitor SpO2 levels. The DC servo motor receives a signal from the microcontroller to engage the ventilator when the sensor registers a SpO2 value below the predetermined threshold. In order to facilitate breathing, the servo motor, which is attached to the ventilator mechanism, changes position. With this configuration, patient safety is improved and immediate medical intervention is made possible by ensuring that the ventilator is promptly engaged in response to significant reductions in SpO2 values.

## LCD Display

**Figure 8.11** 2x16 LCD display

The microcontroller in this health monitoring project is linked to an LCD display to provide vital indications including body temperature, heart rate and SpO2 levels in real time. The microprocessor analyses the data that the sensors gather and updates the LCD panel, making it simple for patients and caregivers to keep an eye on the health metrics all the time.

## Circuit Diagram

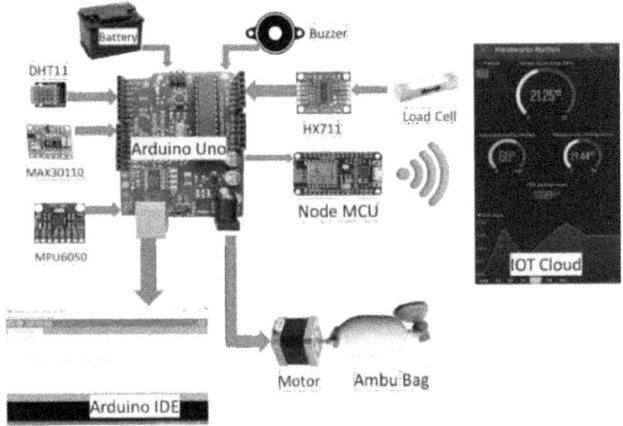

**Figure 8.12** Circuit diagram of proposed system working flowchart

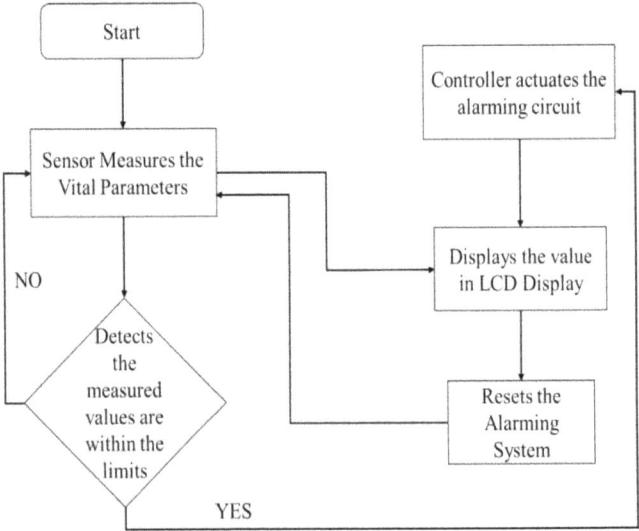

**Figure 8.13** Working flowchart

## Hardware Output

**Figure 8.14** Hardware prototype

## Simulation Output

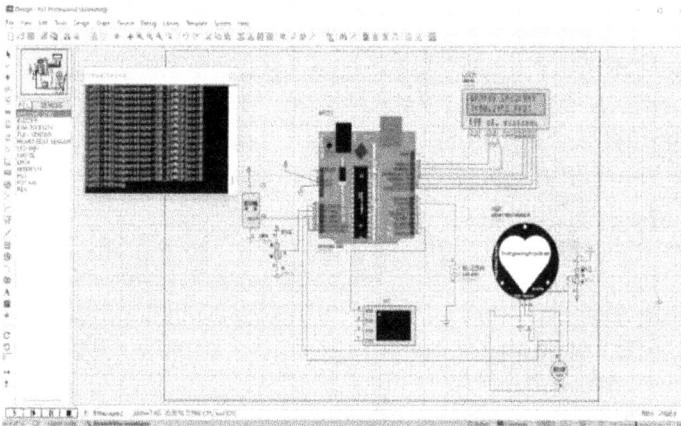

**Figure 8.15** Simulated circuit of the system

## Conclusion

In summary, this study proposes an IoT-based integrated health monitoring and dynamic ventilation control system that marks a substantial leap in healthcare technology. The suggested system provides a complete answer for enhancing patient care in healthcare institutions by smoothly combining a number of sensors, dynamic control mechanisms, and Internet of Things connectivity. We have described the main features and parts of the system in this study, such as the tracking of body temperature, blood oxygen level, heart rate, gyroscopic movement detection, and glucose bottle level monitoring. Together, these sensors monitor important health indicators continually and give medical specialists feedback in real time. All things considered, the suggested IoT-based integrated health monitoring and dynamic ventilation control system has the potential to completely transform patient care by offering individualized, quick, and effective medical treatment.

## References

1.      F. Ullah, M. J. Khan, Q. Arsalan, J. Khattak, U. A. Siddiqui and A. A. Siddiqui, "IoT Platform for Remote Monitoring and Controlling Small-scale Ventilator for SAR Patient," 2023 15th International Conference on Innovations in Information Technology (IIT), Al Ain, United Arab Emirates, 2023.

2.      V. Krishna Prasath, R. Kiruthika Uma, R. Deekshita, T. Arun Prasath and M. Pallikonda Rajasekaran, "Smart Automated Emergency Ventilator (SAEVent): Design of a Low-Cost, Innovative And Portable Ventilator," 2023 9th International Conference on Smart Computing and Communications (ICSCC), Kochi, Kerala, India, 2023.

3.      A. Aziz et al., "Revolutionizing Critical Care: A Smart Positive Pressure Based Non- Invasive Ventilator with Real-time IoT Health Monitoring System," 2023 IEEE 6th International Conference on Knowledge Innovation and Invention (ICKII), Sapporo, Japan.

4.      G. A. Sampedro, J. M. Cobar, K. D. Abaja, R. Baluis, S. L. Huyo-a and M. Abisado, "Smart AmbuBag: A Cloud-Based Automated Respiratory Ventilator," 2022 13th International Conference on Information and Communication Technology Convergence (ICTC), Jeju Island, Korea, Republic of, 2022.

5.      S. Q. Bless, J. K. Abed and M. J. Mnati, "Developing a Portable Smart Ventilator: A Prototype that Balances Cost and Functionality," 2023 7th International Symposium on Innovative Approaches in Smart Technologies (ISAS), Istanbul, Turkiye, 2023.

6.      T. S. Kumar, M. Narendra, U. Arul, S. Kavitha and P. Srinivas, "Design of a Smart Cloud Controlled based Artificial Ventilator Device Controller using Patients Vital Information in a Cloud Data Logs," 2022 Sixth International Conference on I-SMAC (IoT in Social,

Mobile, Analytics and Cloud) (I-SMAC), Dharan, Nepal, 2022.

7.          R. Hossain, R. Shehnil, A. S. Chowdhury, M. S. Mujnebin, M. Hasan and M. R. Uddin, "Design and Development of a Nursing Robot for Non-Invasive Monitoring of Human Body Temperature and Heart Rate," 2023 7th International Conference on Computing, Communication, Control and Automation (ICCUBEA), Pune, India, 2023.

8.     N. Azizah et al., "A Vital Sign Monitoring System Exploiting BT/BLE on Low-cost Commercial Smartwatch for Home Care Patients," 2023 International Seminar on Intelligent Technology and Its Applications (ISITIA), Surabaya, Indonesia, 2023.

9.     P. Sivaranjani, S. Sasikala, S. K, S. M and S.S. R, "IoT Based Smart Ventilator for Automatic Oxygen Flow," 2023 7th International Conference on Trends in Electronics and Informatics (ICOEI), Tirunelveli, India, 2023.

10.     K. Swathi, S. B. Latha, M. N. Vadlamudi,M. A. Alkhafaji, K. S. Mohsen and K. Saikumar, "Automation of Health Monitoring System for Elderly and COVID-19 Patients using IOT," 2023.

# Chapter 9

## Revolutionizing Decision-Making: The Paradigm Shift and Future Applications of Fuzzy Logic

**[1]B. Palpandi, [2]P. Pirabaharan and [3]K. Rajakumar**
[1]Department of Mathematics, University College of Engineering (BIT Campus), Anna University, Tiruchirapalli, Tamil Nadu, India.
[2]Department of Mathematics, Anna University Regional Campus-Madurai, Keelakuilkudi, Madurai, Tamil Nadu, India.
[3]Department of Mathematics, Dhanalakshmi Srinivasan University, Tiruchirapalli, TamilNadu, India.

### Introduction

The Fuzzy logic concept was initially introduced by Lotfi Zadeh in the year of 1965. It is a system of logic that permits for the variation of degrees of truth instead of a traditional binary true/false approach. This approach is more synchronized with the way humans perceive and process information, rectifying uncertainty and imprecision more effectively. Fuzzy logic is having a capability to manage improper data made it relevant in various applications from its inception. Over the span of time, fuzzy logic went through significant advancements. Initially it was applied in control systems and pattern recognition due to its ability to handle the uncertainty; it has now expanded into more complex domains like artificial intelligence and data analysis. The main key developments includes of fuzzy inference systems, fuzzy clustering techniques, and the amalgamation of fuzzy logic with neural networks and genetic algorithms. These advancements have enhanced fuzzy logic's accuracy and effectiveness in modeling and solving complex real-world problems. As compared with fixed binary logic, fuzzy logic is a type of many-valued logic thatdeals with approximate reasoning. It makes use of fuzzy sets, which enable partial truth by allowing items to have degrees of membership ranging from 0 to 1. A temperature of 25°C in an air conditioning system, for instance, can be 20% cold and 80% warm. To these degrees, fuzzy guidelines such as "if warm, then moderate cooling" are applied. The combined data is transformed back into exact commands, like adjusting the cooling amount. Fuzzy logic is utilized in control systems, pattern recognition, and decision-making because it replicates human reasoning by managing ambiguity and imprecision.

## Traditional vs. Modern Approaches in Fuzzy Logic

The initial uses of fuzzy logic were limited to simple tasks, such as functioning cameras and washing machines in residences. These examples showed how fuzzy logic may be used to manage processes more effectively than binary systems.

Fuzzy logic's utilization has been greatly broadened by contemporary methods. Fuzzy logic is currently integrated with deep learning and machine learning to enable complex data processing and decision-making. Furthermore, hybrid systems made up of fuzzy logic and computational intelligence methods like particle swarm optimization and adaptive algorithms are popular. More sophisticated models and more datasets can be correctly handled by these hybrid systems. A significant change in the use of fuzzy logic can be seen in this progression from basic control systems to sophisticated applications in AI and data analytics in current world.

## Challenges in Fuzzy Logic Implementation

The use of fuzzy logic involves several difficulties. The main issue is computational complexity, which can have an exponential impact on scalability as issues get bigger and more complicated. This can lead to a rapid increase in the number of rules and calculation time.

Integrating fuzzy logic with current technologies and systems especially older ones that weren't built for it presents another difficulty. Accurately defining membership functions and rule sets is another skill required for designing fuzzy systems, and it may be time-consuming and error-prone.

Furthermore, although fuzzy logic is effective at handling errors, it can be challenging to convert fuzzy results into highly accurate, practical decisions. Research must continue to provide more effective algorithms, superior integration techniques, and more approachable design tools to meet these problems.

## Paradigm Shifting in Fuzzy Logic

In fuzzy logic, paradigm-shifting indicates an essential shift in the transformation, development, and application of fuzzy logic concepts and methods. This transition usually entails switching from conventional methods to more creative and advanced ones that take into account improvements in principle, technology, and application fields. Fuzzy logic was first mostly employed in consumer electronics and basic control systems, including washing machines and cameras, where it handled imprecision to maintain smooth functioning. Fuzzy logic is used nowadays in increasingly complicated fields including big data analytics, autonomous systems, artificial intelligence, and smart technologies. These applications allow for the application of fuzzy logic to more complex decision-making processes.

Initial to the integration of other computing techniques, early fuzzy logic systems were frequently stand-alone systems that applied fundamental fuzzy rules to control systems. Fuzzy logic is now combined with various computer intelligence methods like neural networks, genetic algorithms, and machine learning. By combining the best features of both approaches, this integration produces hybrid systems that improve accuracy, performance, and adaptability. Although the early fuzzy logic algorithms were simple to use, they might become computationally costly and ineffective when dealing with large-scale issues. More recent algorithms, like type-2 fuzzy logic, rule reduction strategies, clustering approaches, and parallel processing, concentrate on increasing computing efficiency. Fuzzy logic is now more useful in large-scale and real- time applications because to these developments.

Previous approaches handled a limited range of uncertainties due to their basic fuzzy inference mechanisms. To represent complex systems more accurately and to simulate larger levels of uncertainty, modern systems use advanced fuzzy inference techniques such as interval type-2 fuzzy logic. Early uses of fuzzy logic were restricted to domains like pattern recognition  and control systems. Fuzzy logic is used in many different industries nowadays, such as finance (for risk assessment and decision-making), healthcare (for diagnosis and treatment planning), autonomous cars (for navigation and control), and the Internet of Things (IoT) (for managing linked smart devices). In the beginning, the precise definition of membership functions and rule sets was necessary for developing fuzzy systems. A wider range of users without any deep understanding of fuzzy systems can now apply fuzzy logic because of the development of more approachable tools and frameworks.

Recent research focused on verifying fuzzy logic's idea and establishing its fundamentals. Both present and future research endeavors center on optimizing algorithms, enhancing their integration with other technologies, broadening the scope of applications, and tackling obstacles like precision and processing efficiency. Subsequent investigations seek to extend the limits of fuzzy logic by investigating its applicability in developing technology and intricate real-world issues.

Fuzzy logic has undergone a paradigm change that includes the development of advanced computing techniques, integration with modern technology, and departure from its theoretical foundations and basic applications. This change is a reflection of fuzzy logic's continuous development in response to fresh opportunities and problems in today's world.

**Advancements in Fuzzy Logic Algorithms**

Fuzzy logic methods have been improved recently with the goal of improving accuracy, efficiency, and applicability. Type-2 fuzzy logic is a noteworthy advancement that tackles uncertainty in membership functions, enabling more accurate modeling of intricate systems.

Techniques like rule reduction, clustering, and parallel processing areexamples of efforts to minimize computing complexity and make handling large-scale problems easier. Fuzzy logic is now more practical for real-time applications because to these developments.

Adaptive fuzzy systems fuzzy logic combined with machine learning are able to learn from data and dynamically modify their rules. This flexibility is especially useful in dynamic contexts such as financial forecasting, healthcare diagnostics, and autonomous cars.

## Applications of Fuzzy Logic in Various Domains

Considering fuzzy logic can deal with uncertainty and imprecision, it is used in a broad spectrum of applications. Fuzzy logic controllers improve decision-making in industrial and manufacturing processes by optimizing operations and quality control. Fuzzy logic, for example, maintains ideal conditions in steel and cement kilns, enhancing productivity and product quality.Fuzzy logic is used in healthcare to improve diagnosis, treatment planning, and patient monitoring by integrating and analyzing patient data to provide moreprecise and customized care. Since the symptoms and test findings of many diseases, including diabetes, cardiovascular disease, and cancer, frequently overlap, fuzzy logic systems have been employed in their diagnosis. Fuzzy logic is used in finance to evaluate risks, model market patterns, and make investment decisions. Its capacity to interpret ambiguous data is useful for managing portfolios and forecasting market behavior. Fraud detection, stock market analysis, and credit rating are some examples of applications.

## Case Studies of Successful Fuzzy Logic Implementations

The Tokyo subway system, which uses fuzzy logic controllers to control train speed and braking, is a noteworthy case study. Both passenger comfort and energy efficiency have increased because of this application. Fuzzy logic- controlled consumer devices, such as washing machines and cameras, optimize performance in response to many inputs, resulting in improved cleaning or image quality while preserving resources.

Fuzzy logic technologies improve vehicle control and safety in the automobile sector. Fuzzy logic, for instance, is utilized in traction control (TCS) and anti-lock braking (ABS) systems to modify in real-time based on road conditions, enhancing vehicle stability and safety.

## Future Directions and Research Opportunities

Fuzzy logic's integration with cutting-edge technologies is where its futurelies. The Internet of Things (IoT) and fuzzy logic together can handle and comprehend enormous volumes of data from many sources, resulting in systems that are more intelligent and responsive. The use of fuzzy logic in machine learning and artificial intelligence is another exciting field. Fuzzy logic can help AI systems handle uncertainty and make more complex decisions, which will advance industries such as autonomous systems, robotics, and natural language processing. Potential areas of research include developing new algorithms and optimization strategies to increase the computing efficiency of fuzzy systems, which will make them more useful for large-scale, real-time applications. Creating easily navigable tools and frameworks can help encourage broader industry adoption of fuzzy logic.

## References

- Zadeh, L. A. (1965). "Fuzzy sets." *Information and Control*, 8(3), 338-353.
- Ross, T. J. (2004). Fuzzy Logic with Engineering Applications. John Wiley &Sons.
- Mendel, J. M. (2001). Uncertain Rule-Based Fuzzy Logic Systems:Introduction and New Directions. Prentice Hall.
- Li, H., & Yu, L. (2007). "Applications of fuzzy logic in bioinformatics."Artificial Intelligence in Medicine, 41(2), 117-132.
- Wang, L. X. (1994). Adaptive Fuzzy Systems and Control: Design andStability Analysis. Prentice-Hall.
- Pedrycz, W., & Gomide, F. (2007). Fuzzy Systems Engineering: Toward Human-Centric Computing. John Wiley & Sons.
- Zimmermann, H. J. (2010). "Fuzzy set theory." Wiley InterdisciplinaryReviews: Computational Statistics, 2(3), 317-332.
- Kacprzyk, J., & Pedrycz, W. (Eds.). (2015). Springer Handbook of Computational Intelligence. Springer.

# Chapter 10

## Control Techniques of Shunt Active Power Filter to Regulate the DC Link Voltage in Single Phase System

**C. Pearline Kamalini[1], M. V. Suganyadevi[1], N. Gayathri[1] and R.Rekha[2]**
[1]Department of EEE, Saranathan College of Engineering, Trichy, India
[2]Department of Mechanical Engineering, Saranathan College of Engineering, Trichy, India

### Abstract

Electrical power supply quality is an essential problem for both utility providers and end- users, but electromagnetic disruptions can affect the quality. Harmonics is one of the main causes of problems with power efficiency. In power systems that are substantially below the switching frequencyof the filter, active power filters may be used to filter out harmonics. The goal of this work is to develop a shunt Active power filter approach based on a PI controller and Fuzzy logic controller to mitigate theharmonics and reactive power compensation technique for a single-phase non-linear load and to measure the harmonic indices using the MATLAB/SIMULINK model.

**Keywords:** Harmonics, Shunt Active power Filter, PI controller, Fuzzy controller, THD

### 10.1 Introduction

Active Power Filters (APF) stabilizes harmonics by injecting the same frequency of active power but with a reverse step in order to cancel the harmonic [1][4]. Active power filters are electronic power devices dedicated to enhancing the quality and reliability of the usage of electrical energy. Shunt, series, and hybrid are the main Categories for active power filter topologies [2]. As the static compensator (STATCOM) used in the power transmission system, the SHAPF is a self-controlled DC bus. The Shunt Active Power Filter is primarily used to overcome the harmonics of the supply current, for the reactive power generated by non-linearloads in the distribution system. SHAPFs are linked to the power distribution system in parallel and provide low impedance paths to the field. It acts as a current source and injects the current harmonic components provided by the load with 180 degrees out of phase. By the use of active filter the load current harmonic components are cancelled by the use of the active filter and the source current remains sinusoidal and in phasewith the respective to phase to neutral voltage. [3] Shunt Active Filters are widely used and more cost-effective than Series Active Filters. The shunt active filter basic compensation principles are shown in Figure 10.1.

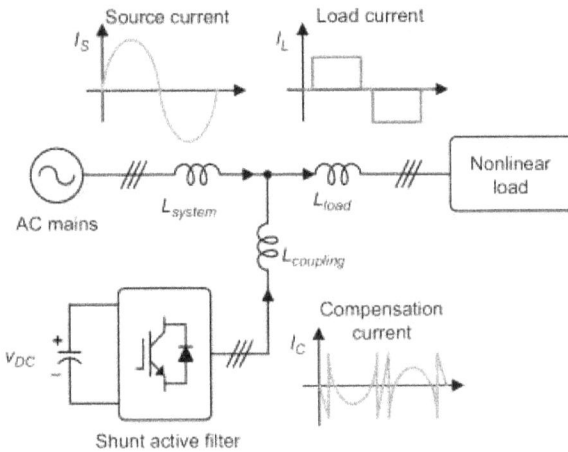

**Figure 10.1** Basic compensation of shunt active power filter

A voltage source inverter (VSI) is used as a shunt active power filter to draw or supply a compensating currentIc from or to the utility, in such a way that it cancels current harmonics on the AC side, i.e. this active powerfilter (APF) induces nonlinearities as opposed to load nonlinearities [5].A constant DC voltage is given by the DC connection capacitor and serves as an energy storage component to provide real power difference during transients between load and source. The actual power supplied in a steady state by the source should be equal to the actual power demand of the load plus some minor power to mitigate the losses in the active filter. The DC connection voltage can therefore be retained at a reference point.

122

## 10.2 Proposed Control Schemes

Regulation of the DC link voltage using

A)    PI Controller

The actual power supplied in a steady state by the source should be equal to the actual power demand of the load plus some minor power to mitigate the losses in the active filter. Consequently, the DC link voltage may be held at a reference value. It will interrupt the real power balance between the mains and the load [6].The DC connection capacitor must compensate for this actual power difference as the load situation shifts. This alters the DC connection's voltage away from the reference voltage. The reference current peak value must be changed in order to maintain a satisfactory operation of the active filter in order to alter the actual power drawn from the source proportionally.

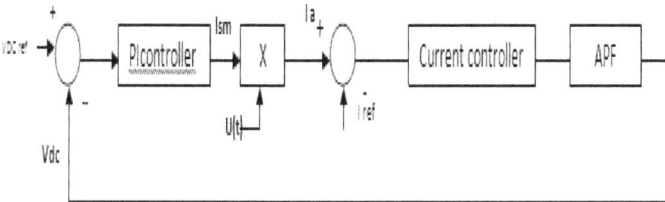

**Figure 10.2** SHAPF with PI controller

In Figure 10.2, the block diagram that senses the dc relation capacitor voltage and compares it to the dc referencevoltage is shown. The voltage error is stored in the PI Controller. The output of the PI controller is the peakvalue of the reference current, multiplied by the vector of the sensed supply voltage unit to produce the current of the unit power factor, and this value is processed in the current controller to generate the gate pulse in APF for the MOSFET [6][7]. The Hysteresis current controller determines the switching pattern ofthe active filter in order to maintain the actual injected current of the filter so as to remain within the optimum hysteresis band (HB) as shown in Figure 10.3.

123

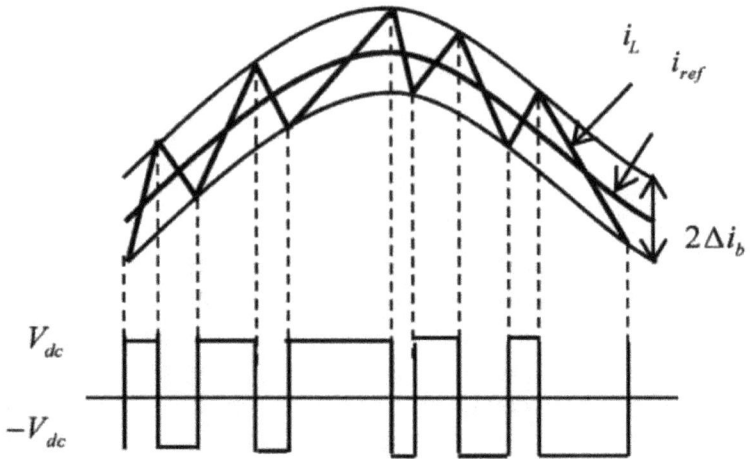

**Figure 10.3** Hysteresis current controller

The switching logic is formulated as follows:
If (ic>ic* + hb) S1'and S2' OFF, S3 'and S4 ' OFF If (ic<ic* -hb) S1'and S2' ON, S3'and S4' ON. Where S1,S2 ,S3,S4 are the switches of APF and HB is the hysteresis bandwidth in amperes. The switching frequency varies along with current waveform. Switching frequency depends upon how fast the current changes from lower limit to upper limit and vice versa. In active filter inductance value determine the filtercurrent to be injected in line.

B)     Fuzzy Logic Controller

A fuzzy inference process consists of the following phase:
Step 1: Fuzzification of input variables Fuzzification
Defuzzification e (n) I max=I max (n-1) + Imax(n) Vdc e (n-1) Vdcref Decision Making 2.
Step 2: Application of fuzzy operator (AND, OR, NOT) in the IF (antecedent) part of the rule.
Step 3: Implication from the antecedent to theconsequent (THEN part of the rules).
Step 4: Aggregation of the consequents across the rules.Step 5: Defuzzification

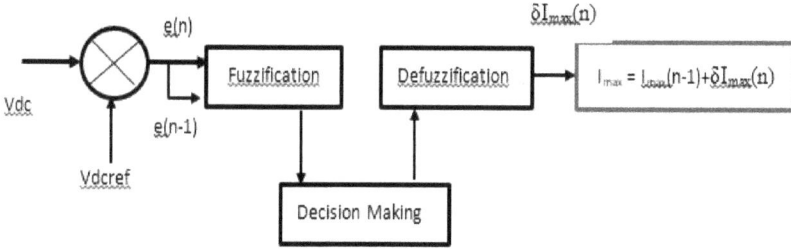

**Figure 10.4** Fuzzy control scheme

The fuzzy control rule architecture involves defining rules that connect the input variables to the output model's properties. The design is focused primarily on the process's intuitive feeling and experience, as FLCis independent of the system model [8]. A revised rule has been implemented based on the system's general complex behavior [9]. The e- error and the Ce- error shift are the FLC's input variables. The output is the shift of a reference current ($\delta$Imax) as shown in Figure 10.4. Figure 10.5 and 10.6 describe the membership function, control rule respectively [10].

| E ＼ ΔE | NL | NM | NS | ZE | PS | PM | PL |
|---------|-----|-----|-----|-----|-----|-----|-----|
| NL | NL | NL | NL | NL | NM | NS | ZE |
| NM | NL | NL | NL | NM | NS | ZE | PS |
| NS | NL | NL | NM | NS | ZE | PS | PM |
| ZE | NL | NM | NS | ZE | PS | PM | PL |
| PS | NM | NS | ZE | PS | PM | PL | PL |
| PM | NS | ZE | PS | PM | PL | PL | PL |
| PL | NL | NM | NS | ZE | PS | PM | PL |

**Figure 10.5** Fuzzy control table

125

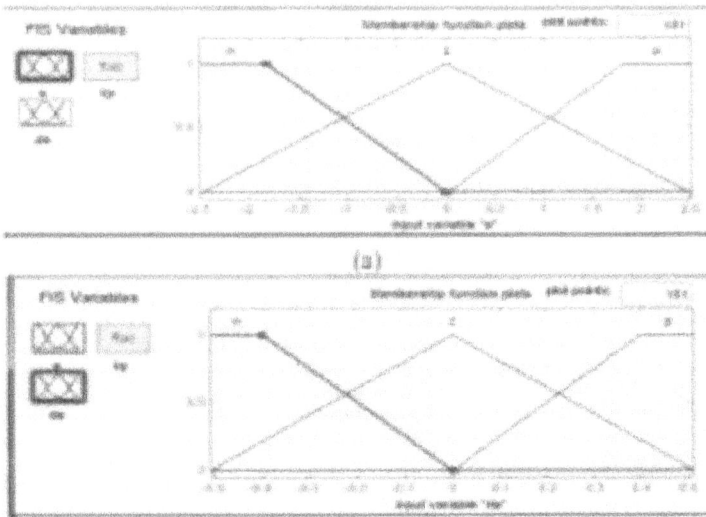

**Figure 10.6** Control rule

## 10.3 Simulation Model

A)     PI controller-based Shunt Active Power Filter

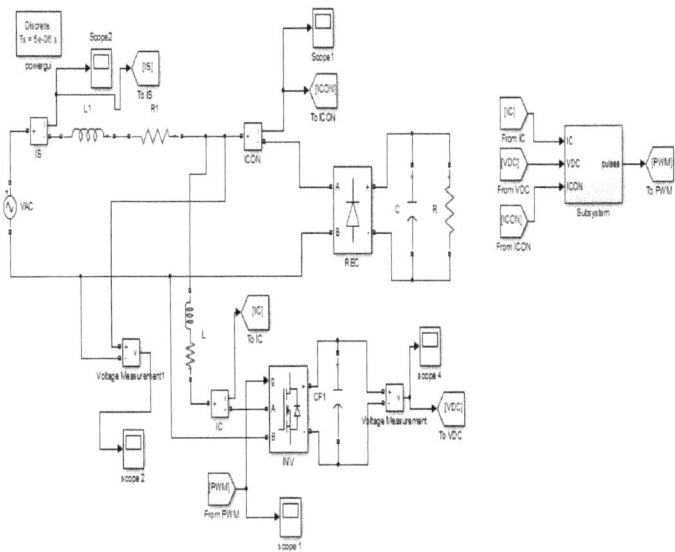

**Figure 10.7** PI controller based SHAPF

B) Fuzzy logic controller-based Shunt Active Power Filter:

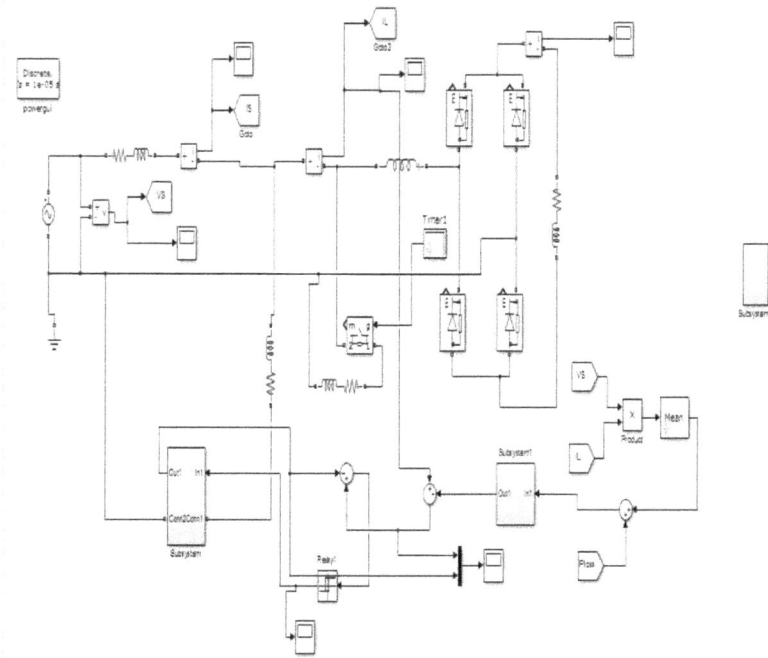

**Figure 10.8** Fuzzy controller based SHPAF

## 10.4 Simulation Results and Analysis

Without the APF and with the APF, the system is simulated. A PI controller and FLC are then used to track the shunt active filter for normal load under a controlled source voltage setting.

A.FFT Analysis of load current without and with SHAPF:

Figure 10.9(a) indicates the usual current trend with non-linear loads without APF. Upon simulation, the corresponding current harmonic spectrum is collected. 83.89 percent of the total current harmonic distortion is found. As seen in Figure 10.9(b), the total load current harmonic with PI controller-based SHAPF is 6.74 percent. The standard non-linear load voltage pattern without SHAPF is seen in Figure 10.10(a) and 26.73 percent of the simple harmonic distortion of the total current is observed.

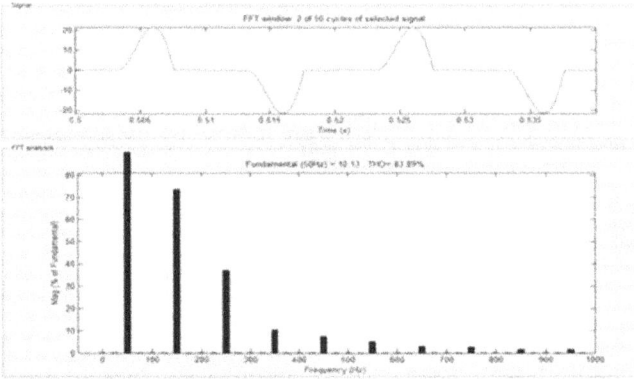

**Figure 10.9(a)**. FFT analysis of load current without SHAPF

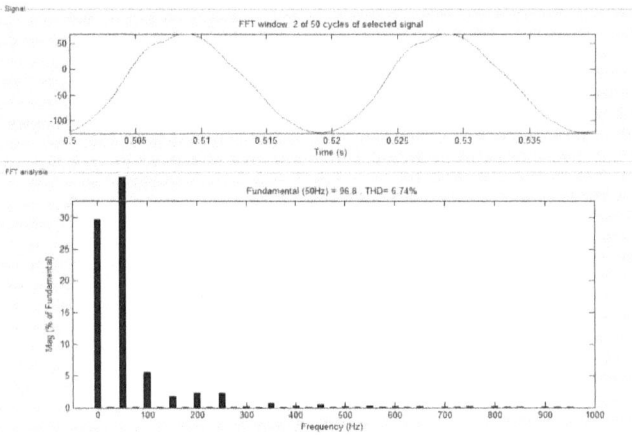

**Figure 10.9(b)**. FFT analysis of load current with PI-SHAPF

128

## B. FFT Load voltage review without and with SHAPF

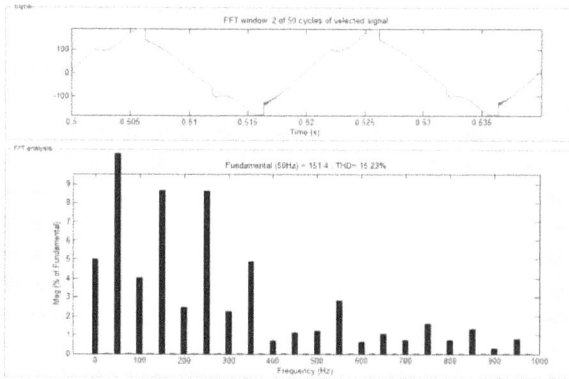

**Figure 10.10(a)**. FFT analysis of load voltage without SHAPF

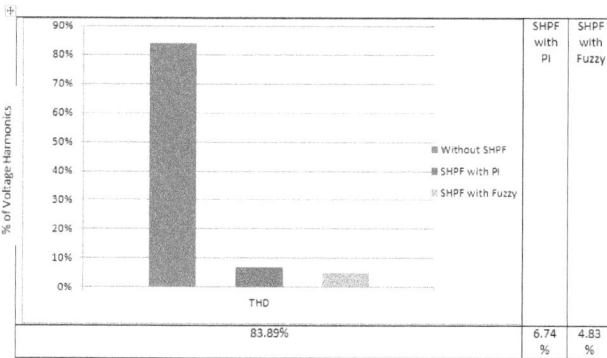

**Figure 10.10(b)**. FFT load voltage review with PI-SHAPF

The standard non-linear load voltage pattern with PI controller-based SHAPF is seen in Figure 10.10(b), and 15.23 percent of the overall current harmonic distortion is observed.

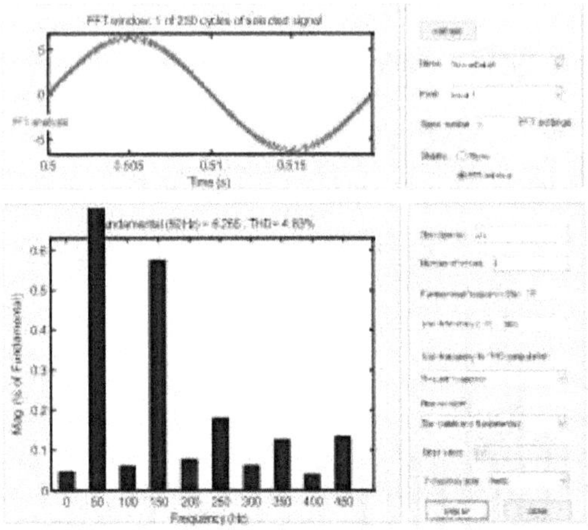

**Figure 10.11** FFT load voltage analysis with the fuzzy controller

The FFT analysis is shown in Figure 10.11 with fuzzy controller-based SHAPF. The total harmonic distortion is obtained as 4.83 percent of the fundamental frequency. Figure 10.12 shows the comparative chart of these PI and Fuzzy logic control techniques.

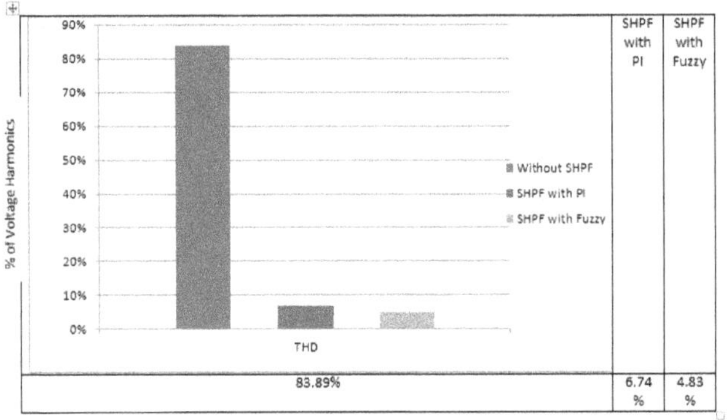

**Figure 10.12** Comparison chart of control techniques

## Conclusion

This article presents the SHAPF simulation model with the PI controller and the Fuzzy controller. The simulation was performed in MATLAB/SIMULINK and the THD value is thus substantially reduced by the implementation of the Shunt Active Power filter and, by compensating for the current harmonics, improves the power efficiency of the device. With the PI controller, the THD of the actual system dropped from the above simulated system to 6.74 percent and from 83.89 percent without the filter to 4.87 percent with the fuzzy controller. According to IEEE519, the THD value should be less than 5 percent and the THD value, depending on the simulated output, is less than 5 percent.

## References

[1]     Zaro, F. O. U. A. D. "Power Quality Improvement using Shunt Active Power Filter: An Industrial ZoneCase Study." *WSEAS Transactions on Power Systems* 18 (2023): 179-185.

[2]     Debdouche, Naamane, Habib Benbouhenni, Brahim Deffaf, Guessabi Anwar, and Laid Zarour. "Predictive direct power control with phase-locked loop technique of three-level neutral point clamped inverter based shunt active power filter for power quality improvement." *International Journal of CircuitTheory and Applications* (2024).

[3]     Gajula, Ujwala, M. Kalpana Devi, and N. Malla Reddy. "Reduced Switch Multilevel Inverter Based Shunt Active Power Filter With ANN Controller for Power Quality Improvement." *Journal of ElectricalSystems* 20, no. 3 (2024): 641-650.

[4]     Iqbal, Mohammed Nadeem, Asini Kumar Baliarsingh, and Pratap Sekhar Puhan. "Power Quality Improvement using a Novel Controller in Shunt Active Power Filter." In *2024 1st International Conference on Cognitive, Green and Ubiquitous Computing (IC-CGU)*, pp. 1-5. IEEE, 2024.

[5]     Kundu, Sombir, Madhusudan Singh, and Ashutosh K. Giri. "SPV-wind-BES-based islanded electrical supply system for remote applications with power quality enhancement." *Electrical Engineering* 106, no. 1 (2024): 279-294.

[6]     M. H J. Bollen, "Understanding Power Quality Problems" in Piscataway, NJ, USA:IEEE Press, 2000.

[7]     Rezapour, Hamed, Farid Fathnia, Mohammad Fiuzy, Hamid Falaghi, and António Mendes Lopes. "Enhancing power quality and loss optimization in distorted distribution networks utilizing capacitors and active power filters: A simultaneous approach." *International Journal of Electrical Power & Energy Systems* 155 (2024):

109590.

[8]     Morán, Luis, Juan Dixon, and Miguel Torres. "Active filters." In *Power Electronics Handbook*, pp. 1301-1341. Butterworth-Heinemann, 2024.

[9 Singh, Bhim, Kamal Al-Haddad, and Ambrish Chandra. "A review of active filters for power quality improvement." *IEEE transactions on industrial electronics* 46, no. 5 (1999): 960-971.

[10]     Li, Dayi, Tingkang Wang, Wenhao Pan, Xinzhi Ding, and Jie Gong. "A comprehensive review ofimproving power quality using active power filters." *Electric Power Systems Research* 199 (2021): 107389.

[11]     Salmeron, Patricio, and Salvador P. Litran. "Improvement of the electric power quality using seriesactive and shunt passive filters." *IEEE transactions on power delivery* 25, no. 2 (2009): 1058-1067.

# Chapter 11

## Hortulanus - Human Following Farm Assistant – Bot

**Danila Shirly A. R, Raymond A., Priadharshni S., Trisha K., Lakshna C.** and **Loubet R.**

### Abstract

Farmers face multiple, complex, and changeable challenges that need diversification of solutions beyond conventional ways of farming. One of the most paramount areas in need of immediate adjustment is the field of harvesting. While machinery and technology have progressed in farming, there are vast areas that are open to new instrumental development, particularly for small and medium-sized farmers. These operations often lack access to specialized equipment tailored to different crop types, resulting in inefficiencies and productivity gaps. Smart sensors and analytics will provide real-time valuable insights to farmers for informed decisions in view of yield and resource optimization. Knowing the losses at the stage of transportation is very critical to ensure the sustainability and economic viability of the farms. Moving further, advanced packaging can be followed, and in this, insulated containers with logistic processes optimized to deleverage the risk to the least and ensure safe and timely arrival at destination. Hence investments in the training and capacity-building programs must target farmers and farm workers to realize the outputs and manage sustainability in the long run. The proposed robot design leaves every place entered by the user for continuous support and assistance and also has the ability to transport some objects for the user across the farm is, by itself, a great enhancement of efficiency and productivity at the farm.

### Introduction

Farmers and gardeners are very important in feeding growing populations and improving the economies of countries. These are very complex issues whose solutions go beyond farming that had been traditionally practiced. One area that deserves immediate attention for change is harvesting. Agriculture has undergone rapid development in terms of machinery and technologies, but at the same time, new tools are needed by small and medium-scale farmers. Most of them lack the necessary specialized equipment related to their specific crops; this generally means inefficiency. Different types of harvesting machines are needed for various crops: soft fruits need gentle handling, while in case of root crops, effective solutions must be found. Smart sensors and analytics provide real-time insights to improve farmers' yields and resource use efficiency. Other automation technologies-robotic harvesters, for example-strive to improve productivity by decreasing dependence on human labor. Minimizing transportation losses is key to farm sustainability and economic viability. Advanced packaging uses thermally insulated containers together with optimized logistics to minimize such risks and ensure timely delivery. IoT tracking enables real-time visibility into consignment location, which offers a proactive quality management system to avoid product loss. The underlying note of knowledge sharing supports collaboration among the stakeholders for innovation. Training programs should be invested in farmers and farm workers to meet the output for sustainability. Addressing food security, economic prosperity, and environmental conservation will result in a resilient and sustainable agricultural future.

## Objectives

Farmers and gardeners form the backbone of our agricultural systems, which play a highly strategic role in feeding populations and sustaining the world's economy. Challenges faced by them, however, remain multidimensional and constantly changing, and their solution calls for innovative moves far beyond classic ways of farming. One of the fundamental areas which demands urgent response and innovation is optimization in the realm of harvesting processes. Yet enormous opportunities still exist for improvement in the sector, which has seen notable progress in agricultural machinery and technology development, particularly in small and medium-sized farms that cannot afford specialized equipment for different crops and are therefore less productive. In the case of strawberries or tomatoes, which are very perishable fruits, they must be handled with great care to avoid being crushed and to keep their freshness for a longer time. On the other side, the harvesting of tubers, such as potatoes or carrots, must be done with proper techniques so that loss is minimized and quality is kept. In this way, farmers using maneuverable harvesting equipment can save valuable time and re-sources, minimizing conceded losses and enhancing profitability. Besides, smart sensors and data analytics integrated into these systems provide real-time valuable information on crop conditions and performance metrics. A data-driven approach empowers farmers to make better decisions on how to adjust harvest parameters or schedules to optimize yields together with resource use. It allows for predictive maintenance of equipment, reducing downtime while enhancing the efficiency of operations as a whole. In addition, labor optimization shows another critical aspect of promoting efficiency in harvesting. Agricultural activities like harvesting are intrinsically labor-intensive and, as a rule, connected with higher labor costs and an insufficient workforce during peak seasons. The automation technologies, including robotic harvesters and automatic picking systems, bring a promise to this challenge. They can work continuously, showing no signs of fatigue, adapt to changing environmental conditions, and perform with greater precision and speed compared to manual work. Investment in automation reduces human labor demand, thereby increasing productivity and profitability in general farming. Other than efficiency in harvesting, addressing the losses that may occur from here up to the point of utilization is a concern to ensure that the entire activity remains sustainable and economically reasonable. Transport is prone to dangers, such as physical damage, changes in temperature, and contamination, which will eventually lead to massive losses and an erosion in market value. These challenges might be managed under adoption of innovative ways of packaging products, use of insulated containers, and improvement of logistical processes for the safe and timely delivery either to the markets or storage. In addition, for the purpose of tracing the location, conditions, and movement of their products in the value chain, farmers apply the use of IoT tracking and monitoring systems. This real-time visibility enables companies to act proactively in the prevention of losses, to maintain product quality, and to optimize the management and distribution of inventory, which can therefore support data-driven decision-making for market demand forecasting and supply chain optimization. The challenges of harvest picking and carrying that would otherwise be enormous, particularly for multi-product farms or for intensive operations, can therefore be alleviated. Picking and carrying are typical means and forms that prove to be time-consuming, labor-intensive, inefficient, and may cause damage to the product. The development of ergonomic tools—creation and adoption of light-weight containers, flexible harvesters, and mechanized transport systems—has different practical cases where several challenges have eased with improvement in efficiency, worker safety, reduction in physical strain, besides making the sector more inclusive and sustainable to agriculture. Additionally, farm management includes cleanliness on the farm and vegetation management. Rough vegetation, withered branches, and other derbies interfere with the operation of factories, cause accidents, and influence productive quantities. Therefore, mechanism qualities of mulching machines, trimming equipment, and robotic mowers ease up management and make the farm environment safe and ordered. The challenges of the industry of agriculture and horticulture need handling in essentially many dimensions in an integrated, comprehensive, and collaborative manner. More efficient harvesting, less loss during transportation, effective carry and handling of farm products by good farm hygiene, and management of vegetation enhance a more resilient and productive agricultural sector. This does not only benefit the farmer and the consumer but also fuels food security, economic outputs, and environmental conservation at the global level.

**Proposed Methodology**

The concept for an agri-support robot has met mixed applause and skepticism from within the agricultural sector. This technology is sure to bring about a transformed phase of farming with the duties of the robot programmed to execute the various daily jobs performed by farmers with ease and speed. In fact, the proposed robot design leaves every place entered by the user for continuous support and assistance. The ability to transport some objects for the user across the farm is, by itself, a great enhancement of efficiency and productivity at the farm. One of the best features of this farm assistant robot is its capability to carry objects for the user. This changes the lives of farmers who have to move heavy and bulky objects across their fields. With the robot by their side, farmers can now do other tasks as this robot does the heavy lifting. This therefore saves a lot of time with decreased exposure of the user's body to heavy tasks, leading finally to minimal fatigue and injuries. The robot also displays carrying capacity, obviating the chance for the user to put it, therefore, in overexertion. Additionally, besides carrying objects for the user, the farming assistant robot is also equipped to aid in their movement on the farm. It is designed to clean the user's path by removing any materials that may otherwise inhibit or slow down the user's progress. This is very essential when traveling over tall grass and uneven terrain. Equipped with advanced sensors, the robot identifies possible obstructions quickly and clears the way, thereby making the user's motion smooth and safe. Besides these, it will also be able to do away with branches from disturbing trees along the traveling track, thus not falling fully on one's shoulders. It saves the individual's time, and the safety of the user is ensured in that the hazard is reduced as much as possible. The other thing that can be incorporated into the farming assistant robot is indicating the weight of the products in the carriage. This is majorly important to farmers needing to have a record of the quantity of produce on the move. The robot's display is mostly an input for the farmer to follow, who is helped to practice farming on an informed ground concerning his yield. This can further help in inventory management since at all times, farmers can know the amount of produce. It also relieves the user of much time, energy, and effort that is spent in weighing manually. This latest technology of the farming assistant robot embeds the advancements made in machine learning and deep learning, very essential in augmenting the robot's AI, data decision-making, and improving its overall performance. ML model enables the robot to learn from experience and optimize navigation paths, predict obstacles, and optimize resources based on historical and real-time sensor inputs. Deep learning models, such as deep neural networks, further empower the perception capability of the robot in distinguishing and classifying objects, understanding user commands, and then making the right decisions based on those visual and audio inputs. Until there is route optimization, collision avoidance, or prioritizing tasks over changing environmental conditions, reinforcement techniques through trial and error remain the driving precept behind the robot learning process. These technologies are embodied within adaptive control systems of farm robots. Changing dynamics and robot parameters make the latter effective to work at different farms, considering continuous performance improvement thanks to self-learning. Indeed, more power for the robot comes through predictive modeling and analyzing data for actionable insights, forecasting trends, and recommending data-driven actions in its contribution towards the optimization of farm operations, enhancement of productivity, and fostering of sustainable agrarian practices in line with the latest technological trends in the sphere. The farm assistant robot will also have AI capabilities through machine learning. This will facilitate learning and adaptation according to the style of the user in farming. All this will predict what the user needs based on the data being collected by movability and action of the user. That personal approach will enhance the user experience and also the robot's performance in due course. AI can aid in bringing forth patterns of the data available on the farm, which can be very informative in making better decisions. The introduction of a farming assistant robot is capable of revolutionizing the agriculture industry. Its mobility and carrying capacity cut the workload of the farmers, which can therefore be utilized in some other significant work. Efficiency measures provided by path cleaning and tree cutting are farm safety measures. Real-time information about weight helps to provide powerful information to the user and great simplification in inventory management. AI features make the robot intelligent and adaptive in farming. So, in conclusion, the development of the proposed farming assistant robot is promising. Its features and capabilities increase the efficiency, productivity, and safety of farming operations. This technology is capable of bringing great changes in the way farmers work and will contribute a lot to the growth of the agriculture industry as a whole. As this new innovative technology is integrated, the future is bright and the beginning of an exciting time for farmers. It is endless, and possibilities might earn the farming assistant robot a future as a very important device in modern agricultural implements.

## Circuit Connections

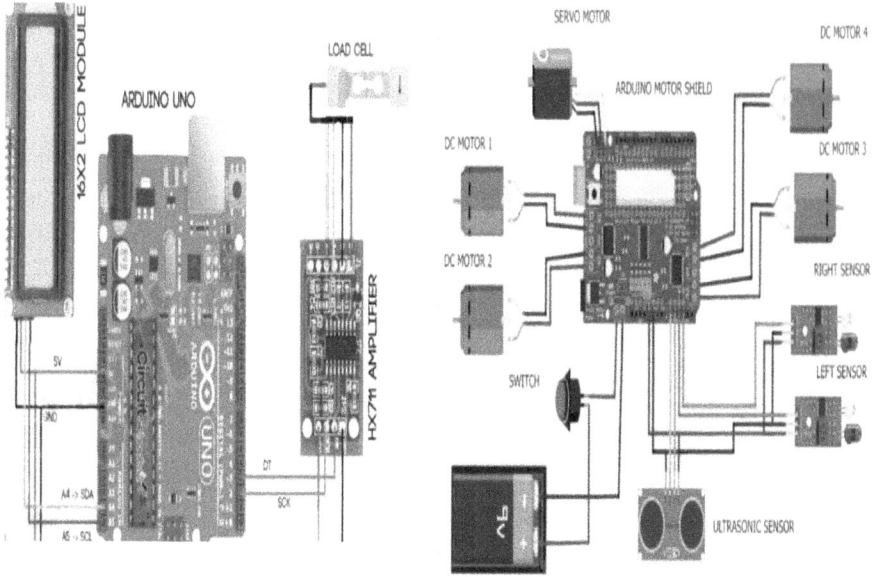

## Results

## Conclusion

A system of human-following robots will assist human farmers in the implementation of tracking algorithms. This will allow precise location and following of gardeners or farmers within farms and gardens, with obstacle avoidance incorporated to ensure safety for both humans and the robot from any disasters or disruptions in the farm environment.

## References

1. D. F. Gias and T. Kanda, "Simultaneous People Tracking and Localization for Social Robots Using External Laser Range Finder", *IEEE/RSJ Int. Conf on Intelligent Robotics and Systems*, pp. 846-853, 2009.
2. Harshad Done and Pratik Chopra, *Department of Electrical Engineering 'VOICE Operated ROBOT' K. J. Somaiya College of Engineering*, 2006-2007.
3. Javed Aquib Khan, "Wireless Gesture-Controlled Robot", January 2015.
4. Michael Moran, "Robotic Arm Evolution", *March 2013 International Journal of Advanced Electronics and Communication Engineering Research*.
5. Peter Bajku, Martin Urban and Jean Chistophen, "Detection of hand movements using multiple sensors", *Lementec2004 IEEE Conference on Intelligent Transportation Systems*, October 4, 2004.
6. Gregory Jokin and Dudek Gregory Michael, Robotics' Computational Concepts, Cambridge, UK:The Press Syndicate of Cambridge University, 2000.
7. To M. Cristou, A. And Ohya and S. Yunta, "Person verification detected and based on omni directional variation", *RO-MAN 2011 IEEE*, pp. 419-424, 2011.
8. J. Cai and T. Matsunaru, "Robot Human-following Limited Speed Control", *The 22nd IEEE Int. Symposium Human Interactive Communication (Ro-Man2013)*, pp. 81-86, 2013.
9. L. Ching, "Design and Implementation of Robot Interactive Demonstration System Based on Kinect", *Chinese Control and Decision Conf*, pp. 971-975, 2012.
10. M. Cao, H. Hashimuto and E. Nachida, "Motion sensor Robot with Kinetic 3D Sensor", *SICE Annual Conf*, pp. 2207-2211, 2012.

www.ingramcontent.com/pod-product-compliance
Lightning Source LLC
Chambersburg PA
CBHW050502190326
41458CB00005B/1395